LIVING ON THE EDGE

THE REAL GOD

How He Longs for You to See Him

WORKBOOK

The Real God: How He Longs for You to See Him Workbook

© 2017 by Living on the Edge and Chip Ingram

Published by Living on the Edge
P.O. Box 3007
Suwanee, GA 30024

All rights reserved. No part of this publication may be reproduced, stored in a retrieval system, or transmitted in any form or by any means without the prior written permission of the publisher.

Unless otherwise indicated, Scripture is taken from the Holy Bible, New International Version®. NIV®. Copyright© 1973, 1978, 1984 by Biblica, Inc.™ Used by permission of Zondervan. All rights reserved worldwide. www.zondervan.com.

Scripture marked NASB is taken from the New American Standard Bible® copyright© 1960, 1962, 1963, 1968, 1971, 1972, 1973, 1975, 1977, 1995 by The Lockman Foundation. Used by permission. www.lockman.org

Printed in the United States of America.

Special thanks to Dr. Bill Miller and Dr. Timothy Dalrymple of Polymath Innovations.

About Living on the Edge

Living on the Edge exists to help Christians live like Christians. The ministry was established in 1995 as a radio ministry of pastor and author Chip Ingram, and has since grown into an international discipleship ministry. The ministry creates biblical teaching and tools that challenge and equip spiritually hungry Christians to become mature disciples of Jesus.

The ultimate vision of Living on the Edge is to be a catalytic movement of Christians living out their faith in ways that transform families, churches, and communities for the common good and the glory of God.

Chip Ingram

If there's one thing I've learned about people, it's the fact that we all long for the fulfillment that comes from a close, intimate relationship with God. Some may have become deluded by false philosophies, blocked Him out of their lives, or simply become distracted by other things. But underneath it all, God has created each of us with an innate desire for deep, meaningful fellowship with Him.

Believe it or not, that desire lives deep inside you right now. You may not feel it very strongly at this moment, but it's there. Perhaps it's a faint memory, but the longing remains. You may have learned to divert that desire to other things over the years, but you cannot squelch it completely. It is the key to finding purpose in a life that can seem overwhelming on some days and absolutely meaningless on others.

Through this workbook and in reflecting on God's Word, I hope you will begin to feel that desire rekindled and fanned into a flame, perhaps for the first time.

Your journey is about to begin. I pray that you will discover how God longs for you to see Him!

LivingontheEdge.org

Table of Contents

I	Seeking God	6
II	Goodness of God	18
III	Sovereignty of God	34
IV	Holiness of God	48
V	Wisdom of God	64
VI	Justice of God	82
VII	Love of God	100
VIII	Faithfulness of God	118
IX	Conclusion	134

Guide

Welcome to the journey! As you progress through this Workbook you will encounter four different types of activities. Take your time on each one. Remember, the more you seek God, the more He will reveal Himself to you!

Big Picture
A quick introduction to the topic of the chapter.

Video
Watch a 30 minute message from Chip Ingram and record your notes.

Discussion
Discuss the video with friends and family; if studying alone you can answer the questions for yourself.

Next Steps
Dig deeper into the chapter topic and then record the next steps you plan to take.

INDIVIDUAL
Simply follow the activities in the workbook; you may wish to skip over the group discussion questions.

GROUP
Watch Chip videos in advance or together as a group and then discuss; complete the workbook on your own.

CHAPTER ONE

Seeking God

With whom, then, will you compare God?
To what image will you liken him?

Isaiah 40:18

Are You Ready for a Truly Awesome Experience?

BIG PICTURE

Not the shallow kind of awe you might feel when you see a film laden with incredible special effects. Nor the how-do-they-do-that amazement that comes from watching an amazing athlete, artist, or musician.

We mean an authentic, old-fashioned awe. The kind of awe that shakes you to the core. The kind of awe that you feel when you realize that your very existence is sustained in every single moment by the Creator of the universe. The kind of awe you feel in the presence of an Almighty God who governs everything from the stars in the heavens to the smallest details in our lives. The kind of experience that leaves you speechless.

How do you prepare yourself for **that**? There is only one way. Humble your heart.

Moses' example is noteworthy in this regard. He was characterized, perhaps most of all, by humility (Numbers 12:3). In humility He knew God—really knew God—perhaps more than any single individual in human history with the exception of Jesus Himself. Notice what we are told about Moses:

The LORD would speak to Moses face to face, as a man speaks with his friend.
- Exodus 33:11

This study is all about getting to know God better. And that may feel like a daunting task.

Like Moses, we should be humbled. Not because God is hard to know, but because God can (and should) be intimidating. And yet, the Bible informs us that God is a person. He is a "you" and not an "it." So getting to know God, in some ways, ought to be like getting to know any other person. When you learn someone's height and weight, hair color and eye color, do you really know him? Of course not. Getting to know a person involves a process of learning what he loves and hates, hopes and values, thinks and does. It takes time together. It takes communication. He speaks to you; and you reply.

But getting to know God is not exactly the same as getting to know your neighbor. Getting to know another human being almost always involves that person getting to know you as well. As we come to know others, we also come to be known by them—and sometimes they will reject us as they become more familiar with our faults.

With God, however, He already knows you fully. You have no need to fear rejection. He is eager to be known by those who are eager to know Him.

As for you, how passionate are you to know Him? Are you as hungry to know Him as He is hungry to be known?

CHAPTER ONE

How Do You Really View God?

The experience you're about to have with *The Real God Workbook* will guide you through a process of seeing and knowing Him for who He really is. That might seem like an unrealistic promise. Be assured, if you seek to know Him better, He will reveal Himself.

Let's start our journey by considering an everyday life scenario:

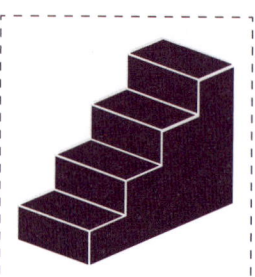

*You are walking at a brisk pace as you approach a set of stairs, anxious about arriving late. They're just ordinary stairs. You would never give them a thought ever again—**until your foot slips off that step.***

In a moment you find yourself falling. The stairs wheel around you in what seems like slow motion. The next instant there's a searing pain in your knee and you know this can't be good. Several hours later, you're leaving the emergency room wondering how your day ended up like this.

What if this were you? What would your thoughts about God be as you left the hospital with a shattered knee—your whole life inconvenienced for months. What feelings and emotions might you have toward Him?

Which of these might be your response in that situation?

- "Are you punishing me for something?"
- "I guess You didn't want me to go to that meeting."
- "It was cool how You had that nurse right there to see what happened and to help me."
- "Why didn't you protect me?"
- "Now at least I know what it's like to ride in an ambulance."

Often our responses to life's circumstances reveal how we think about God, whether it's falling down stairs, getting a promotion, or discovering that your child has a learning disability.

Let's think about this a little deeper by moving away from a random example to your own life. On your right is an exercise to help you reflect further on how you really view God. Over the next few minutes challenge yourself to honestly consider how you think about Him.

Identify one memorable or unexpected moment (good or bad) from the last week or month. This could be something as dramatic as a car accident or as ordinary as finding a $20 bill under the front seat of your car. Then, consider what your thoughts about God were at that moment.

Memorable or unexpected moment	Your thoughts about God in that moment

Reflecting on what you wrote in the exercise, maybe you're encouraged.

On the other hand, maybe you didn't think about Him at all or had thoughts that were not what you wished they had been. As a result you might feel guilty or disappointed in yourself. If so, you're not alone.

> *What you think about God shapes your whole relationship with Him. In addition, what you believe God thinks about you determines how close you will grow toward Him.*
> **- Chip Ingram, The Real God**

What you need to know, however, is that God longs for you to know Him for who He really is.

CHAPTER ONE

Watch Chip Ingram's Teaching and fill in the notes below.

▶ **Seeking God**

> *What comes into our minds when we think about God is the most important thing about us... We tend by a secret law of the soul to move toward our mental image of God.*[1]
> **- A.W. Tozer, *Knowledge of the Holy***

Three facts to consider

1. God is not _____ _____ . *Isaiah 40:25-28; Romans 11:33*

2. Left to ourselves, we tend to _____ God to

_____ _____ . *Romans 1:21-23; Exodus 32:1-6*

3. God can only be known as He _____ _____ to us.

    Through   a) _____ *Psalm 19:1-2; Romans 1:19-20*

                     b) _____ _____ *John 1:1-4; 5:37-40*

                       c) _____ *John 1:14-18; Hebrews 1:1-3*

One question for you

What must I do to see the real God as He really is?

    Answer = _____ _____ *Jeremiah 29:11-14a*

    How? = *Proverbs 2:1-5*

---

[1] Tozer quote: AW Tozer, Knowledge of the Holy, 1961. Both quotes are P1.

CHAPTER ONE

DISCUSSION

Seeking God

The following questions will help you reflect on what you watched on the video. If you are in a group spend some time sharing with others.

1. At the beginning of the video Chip asked "what comes into your mind when you think about God?" My current image of God is _____.

2. Over the years, how has your view of God changed? What prompted the change?

3. How could a distorted view of God impact your everyday life?

4. One of the ways that God has revealed Himself is through His Son, Jesus. To get a picture of this, read John 1:1-5 and 1:14-18. What most stands out to you from these verses? Why?

5. Chip said that the key to knowing the "Real God" is to seek Him. As you think about your pursuit of God, where would you honestly place yourself on the following scale? Share your answer with your group.

1	2	3	4	5	6	7	8	9	10
Not on My Radar									**Passionately Seeking**

   ○ What is one barrier that can keep you from seeking God?

6. Proverbs 2:1-5 provides us with some practical ways that we can seek God. Which one of these statements is something you need to apply in your own life? What would that look like practically?

   My son, if you accept my words and store up my commands within you, turning your ear to wisdom and applying your heart to understanding— indeed, if you call out for insight and cry aloud for understanding, and if you look for it as for silver and search for it as for hidden treasure, then you will understand the fear of the Lord and find the knowledge of God.

As you wrap up your group time, spend a few minutes praying together. Claim God's promise that if we seek Him we will find Him. Honestly share where you are in seeking God and express your desire to know God more deeply.

Preparing to Seek God with Your Whole Heart

This next section is for you to complete on your own. Take what you have learned and turn it into action.

Chip's message challenges us to seek God with our whole hearts. Maybe you are asking yourself:

Am I doing that now? How would I know?

Four Evidences of Knowing God

Start by evaluating where things stand in your own pursuit of knowing God. The exercise below draws upon the categories developed by theologian J.I. Packer in his classic book, *Knowing God*. As a result of his study of the book of Daniel, Packer identified four areas of evidence that show how deeply a person knows God for who He really is.

Packer's four evidences[2] with a brief description of each are listed below. Take a moment to rate yourself for each of the evidences from 1-5, with 5 being the highest.

Rating	Evidence of Knowing God
	Amount of energy for God Those who really know God take action and demonstrate initiative both in public and private as a result of knowing Him.
	Greatness of thoughts about God Those who really know God fill their minds often with awe-inspiring reminders of God's greatness.
	Degree of boldness for God Those who really know God don't hesitate to obey by faith even when it might cost them.
	Level of contentment in God Those who really know God experience peace even in the midst of trying circumstances.

---

2 Pg 5: Four Evidences (JI Packer): These four evidences are taken from Real God chapter 3.

Assessing the Four Evidences in Your Own Life

Continue your self-evaluation by looking at the degree to which these four evidences are exhibited in your life. Make some notes of how you see evidence in that area lacking or showing up in your life. Use the column in the table below to record your observations.

Provide as much specific evidence as you can from personal experience in the boxes on the following page so that you have an accurate picture of your starting point in this study. This will help you evaluate ways that you want to see growth in the weeks ahead as you explore God's **attributes*** and seek to know Him more.

	Evidence where this is lacking in my life	Evidence where this is prevalent in my life
Amount of energy for God		
Greatness of thoughts about God		
Degree of boldness for God		
Level of contentment in God		

attribute, noun. A feature or characteristic of someone or something.

Now that you've completed the evaluation, let's consider how your areas of weakness might result from a flawed or distorted perception of God. The real God overflows all our attempts to constrict Him or control Him. He is so much greater than we can imagine. Yet there is a natural human tendency to reduce "God" to categories we can understand, or twist our image of God in ways that serve our interests.

Perhaps you don't think much about God's greatness because you tend to have a "salad bar" conception of God discussed in the video.

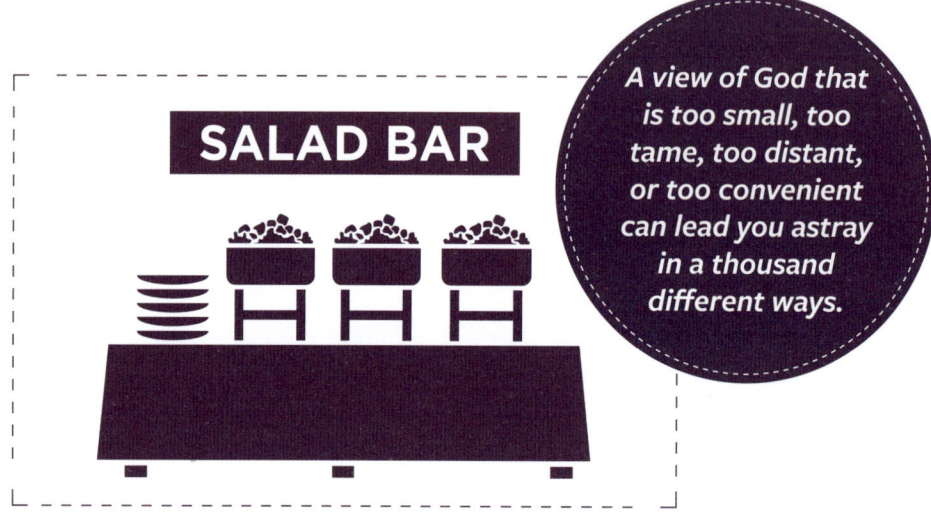

A view of God that is too small, too tame, too distant, or too convenient can lead you astray in a thousand different ways.

Salad Bar Concept of God

Sometimes people construct a false image of God in their minds by picking and choosing from various ideas about God that they have come across in their life experience or develop in their own imagination. Thus, God is limited to a person's preferences and ability to understand. This is in contrast to a biblical concept of God that relies on Scripture to reveal who God is, recognizing that some aspects of God are so vast and different that we cannot comprehend the whole of who God is.

Assessing Your Perception of God

Answer the questions on the next page and seek an honest assessment of how you conceive of God. Again, we all struggle with tendencies to shape an image of God that serves our preferences and presuppositions. This is not meant to be an exercise to beat yourself up. Rather, it's designed to help you see the tendencies in your life to view God in false or distorted ways.

(**Note:** *It is the work of the Holy Spirit to illuminate us. Pray before doing this exercise that God would reveal ways in which your vision of Him needs correction.*)

- **In what ways do you tend to view God as too small?**

  _____
  _____
  _____

- **In what ways do you tend to reduce God to manageable terms?**

  _____
  _____
  _____

- **In what ways do you tend to understand God by ways other than how He reveals Himself in nature, His Word and through His Son?**

  _____
  _____
  _____
  _____

What's the point of all this self-evaluation? Hang in there. We're not indulging in busy work here. It's all for the goal of knowing God—more fully, more accurately, and more intimately.

False or distorted perceptions of God dull our enthusiasm for God, put distance between us and our Creator, and even lead us to behave in ways that are unbiblical.

Therefore, we should continue to ask God to guide us as we strive to correct our vision of Him.

The Bible consistently encourages us that those who seek God will find Him. God wants to be found. God longs for you to know Him. He did, after all, go to great lengths to reveal Himself in Jesus Christ and throughout His Creation. But we only know God to the extent that He reveals Himself to us. The knowledge of God is a gift of grace. So even as we seek Him in our study of God's Word, we should seek Him in prayer and ask Him to make Himself known to us as He truly is.

Seeking God With All Your Heart

Let's identify some very specific steps you can take this week to "seek God with all your heart" (Jeremiah 29:13). As described in the video, Proverbs 2:1-5 provides a helpful framework to identify practical steps for seeking God. We looked at these verses in the Discussion section, but now pause and take a deeper look.

> *My son, if you accept my words and store up my commands within you, turning your ear to wisdom and applying your heart to understanding, and if you call out for insight and cry aloud for understanding, and if you look for it as for silver and search for it as for hidden treasure, then you will understand the fear of the LORD and find the knowledge of God.*
> **- Proverbs 2:1-5**

Note the instructions in these verses:

- **Take the initiative:** Commit that you will join the lifelong quest to know God deeply and truly. Though God is at work, you're not meant to be passive.

- **Be teachable:** Prepare to learn and receive wisdom and understanding about who God is – even if God challenges some of your perceptions of who He is!

- **Pray passionately:** Express in prayer your desire to know Him. Speak out your desire with a genuine heart.

- **Make knowing God your priority:** Knowing God will transform your life in powerful ways. Make it the uttermost aim of your life, above all other interests or concerns.

As you wrap up, make a list of up to three specific things you will commit to do this week to know God better. Develop this list in light of the instructions in Proverbs 2 and the personal areas of weakness you discovered in your self-evaluation.

1 _____

2 _____

3 _____

Putting Your Response to God in Prayer

As you take these specific steps this week, reflect on how it affects your energy for God and the three other areas from Packer's litmus test for knowing God. Knowing God will be your mission in the next seven weeks (and for a lifetime ahead).

In the space below, write out a prayer to God expressing your desire to seek Him and know Him in new and life-changing ways in the coming weeks. It's appropriate to share just a few words about writing out prayers to God before you start.

The goal is to express to God in your own words your desire for Him to show Himself to you as He really is—for Him to correct any distorted impressions you have of Him and give you a view of Him that's in perfect focus. Of course, our prayers to God ought to express proper respect for our Creator. However, don't try to craft perfect sentences to impress God. Just simply express what's in your heart to Him. Below is a sample to help give you an idea of what a written prayer might look like. Under this prayer, write your own prayer to God.

God I know that my view of You is not always right and I admit that I often take You and all that You give me for granted. I'm so sorry. But I want to really know You. I want to be so amazed at who You are that I can't stop thinking about You. Please help me to see You clearly so that I have a healthy fear and respect for You. Please show me ways that I have a distorted view of who You are. And please make me more and more who You want me to be as a result of knowing You more and more each day.

CHAPTER TWO
Goodness of God

Everyone who drinks this water will be thirsty again, but whoever drinks the water I give him will never thirst. Indeed, the water I give him will become in him a spring of water welling up to eternal life.

John 4:13-14

CHAPTER TWO

Walking in the Front Door

BIG PICTURE

Mark remembers the day Jake first walked through the front door. He was so excited to pour his life into this boy. From that first moment, he was all in—ready to give anything to give Jake the very best life.

He knew that Jake was wounded from his experiences growing up in foster care. He knew there would be tough days ahead, but he had no doubts. There would be no changing his mind or his heart. He was completely committed.

Of course, the tough days did come. Jake tested their house rules, lashing out with sarcasm, and withdrew for days at a time from any conversation with Mark and his wife.

But both Mark and his wife remained undaunted. They gave Jake the best they knew to give. They provided a private tutor, fees for a soccer team, and a trip to their church's summer camp, as well as loving discipline and correction.

Mark remained steadfast in his commitment. He knew that Jake still struggled with being part of their family. That didn't change Mark. He would continue to give his very best for Jake.

Jake remembers the day he first entered the door to this house. These people had so much; they were so excited about him. But he was skeptical—and for good reason. "They must want something from me," he thought. Frankly, he hadn't known what to think. He was, after all, only 12 years old at the time.

Jake also remembers before that time. There were plenty of foster homes in his past. He wasn't even sure he could remember them all. Mostly, he just wanted to forget. Bullies. Punishments. Loneliness.

Now, a year after walking through that front door, Jake still doesn't know what to think of Mark and his wife. It only took a few "problems" and then their true colors began to show: prioritizing church over soccer, groundings, and limits on screen time. How many times had he heard, "we just want what's best for you..."?

No matter how many times they say they are committed to him, he has reasons to doubt. As he sits on the living room couch staring at the front door, he wonders, "Do they really care about me? Do they want what's good for me?"

THE REAL GOD WORKBOOK | *Living On The Edge*

19

Even when embraced by such a well-intentioned caregiver, adapting to a new family can be a confusing time for a child like Jake. Many older foster and adopted children initially distrust their caregiver or adoptive parents—and can for many years. The same is true with us. We have been rescued by a loving Father and brought into His household. But if we are really honest with ourselves, we all carry some form of painful baggage: feelings of rejection, fear, disappointment, and loneliness. All of *that* can lead to distrust.[1]

Deep down, do you struggle with distrust? Do you sometimes wonder:

What if God doesn't really want what is best for me?

Can He Be Trusted?

Jake will never fully experience the goodness of Mark and his wife if he can't get past his distrust of them. He will continue to deal with uncertainty, fear, anxiety, or even depression. These will, in turn, influence his responses to their authority in his life.

Does a lack of trust in God's goodness contribute to insecurity, fear, or anxiety in your life too? Do you find these attitudes and feelings in yourself? *(Mark all that apply)*

- ◯ Uncertainty when facing major decisions
- ◯ Fear of punishment for my sins or mistakes
- ◯ Worry that bad things will happen to me or my loved ones
- ◯ Anxiety that God will withhold good things to test me
- ◯ Suspicions that I'm just one of countless, insignificant pawns of God
- ◯ Disobedient or rebellious impulses push back against God's rules
- ◯ Depression from lack of hope for my future
- ◯ Other: _____

There were good reasons for Jake to distrust when he came through that front door for the first time. However...

What if over time Jake discovers that Mark and his wife really are good? What if they really do care for Jake and want the very best for him?

The same is true in your relationship with God. Because God really is good, it can be different. If you can see God for who He really is, you can begin to move beyond distrust to know and feel His goodness and then boldly live with faith in the goodness of God. Let's examine how different—and how good—that can be.

---

[1] Studies showing impact of parental involvement: Some examples of studies: ohttps://www.ncbi.nlm.nih.gov/pmc/articles/PMC2973328/ohttp://patient.info/print/2573ohttps://artifactsjournal.missouri.edu/2014/08/parental-divorce-and-student-academic-achievement/ P

CHAPTER TWO

Watch Chip Ingram's Teaching and fill in the notes below.

▶ The Goodness of God

> "The goodness of God is that which disposes Him to be kind, cordial, benevolent, and full of good will toward men. He is tenderhearted and of quick sympathy... By His nature He is inclined to bestow blessedness and He takes holy pleasure in the happiness of His people."[2]
>
> **- A.W. Tozer, Knowledge of the Holy**

The Battle: _____

The Barrier: _____

The Breakthrough: _____

Thesis: Our distorted view of God is the root of all our problems.

Process: A devotional study of select attributes of God.

How Does God Reveal His Goodness?

Through _____. *Psalm 145:7-9, 16-17*

Through _____. *Psalm 107*

Through _____.

Jesus is the _____ of God's goodness. *Romans 5:8*

Jesus is the _____ of future goodness. *Romans 8:32*

---

2 W Tozer, Knowledge of the Holy, 1961, p82.

CHAPTER TWO

Responding to God's Goodness

1. _____ and receive God's greatest good gift of eternal life through Jesus Christ. *Romans 2:4*

2. _____ your life and future fully to the lordship of Christ. *Romans 12:1*

3. _____ God's promise that you will never miss out on any good thing as long as you live. *Psalm 84:11*

The Goodness of God

The following questions will help you reflect on what you watched on the video. If you are in a group spend some time sharing with others.

1. Chip said, "I falsely assumed that God did not have my best interests at heart and that a deeper commitment to Him would likely result in my missing the things I wanted most."

    o Share a time in your life when you found it difficult to trust in the goodness of God.

2. Read Matthew 7:7-12. As you think about God's goodness, what most stands out to you from this passage?

    "Ask and it will be given to you; seek and you will find; knock and the door will be opened to you. For everyone who asks receives; the one who seeks finds; and to the one who knocks, the door will be opened.

    "Which of you, if your son asks for bread, will give him a stone? Or if he asks for a fish, will give him a snake? If you, then, though you are evil, know how to give good gifts to your children, how much more will your Father in heaven give good gifts to those who ask him! So in everything, do to others what you would have them do to you, for this sums up the Law and the Prophets."

3. From your experience, what can help you trust in God's goodness even when life doesn't seem "good"? Can you think of any biblical examples of people who embraced God's goodness even when life was coming unraveled?

4. A.W. Tozer said, "The goodness of God is that which disposes Him to be kind, cordial, benevolent, and full of good will toward men. He is tenderhearted and of quick sympathy... By His nature He is inclined to bestow blessedness and He takes holy pleasure in the happiness of His people."

    o   What word or phrase most stands out to you? What word or phrase do you have a hard time really believing?

5. Read Psalm 145:3-9. The Psalmist says in verse 9 that "The Lord is good to all." Spend a few minutes as a group sharing different ways you have experienced God's goodness.

    Psalm 84:11 says:
    For the Lord God is a sun and shield;
    the Lord bestows favor and honor;
    no good thing does he withhold
    from those whose walk is blameless.

    o   How do the words sun, shield, favor, and honor reflect the goodness of God?

As you conclude your group time, spend time praying together and thanking God for His goodness. Read Psalm 34:1-10 and use the words and phrases of this Psalm to express your heart of gratitude to God.

CHAPTER TWO

NEXT STEPS

God's Goodness Revealed in Scripture

This next section is for you to complete on your own. Take what you have learned and turn it into action.

In order to deepen your understanding of God's goodness, we are going to look at several passages of Scripture. After reading them through a few times, write your response to the question in the box just below the verse. For the first verse, a sample response is provided.

He causes his sun to rise on the evil and the good, and sends rain on the righteous and the unrighteous.
- Matthew 5:45

- **How does this passage affirm or inform your understanding of the goodness of God?**

    God provides for the basic needs of both the righteous and the unrighteous. He doesn't hold back good things like sun and rain from the unrighteous, but "causes" the sun to shine on them and "sends" rain to all people.

They will celebrate your abundant goodness and joyfully sing of your righteousness. The LORD is gracious and compassionate, slow to anger and rich in love. The LORD is good to all; he has compassion on all he has made.
- Psalm 145:7-9

- **How does this passage affirm or inform your understanding of the goodness of God?**

> **❝**
> *Give thanks to the LORD, for he is good; his love endures forever...*
> *Then they cried out to the LORD in their trouble, and he delivered*
> *them from their distress.*
> - **Psalm 107:1,6**

- **How does this passage affirm or inform your understanding of the goodness of God?**

_____

_____

_____

_____

> **❝**
> *As Jesus started on his way, a man ran up to him and fell on his knees before him. "Good teacher," he asked, "what must I do to inherit eternal life?" "Why do you call me good?" Jesus answered. "No one is good—except God alone."*
> - **Mark 10:17-18**

- **How does this passage affirm or inform your understanding of the goodness of God?**

_____

_____

_____

_____

> *Every good and perfect gift is from above, coming down from the Father of the heavenly lights, who does not change like shifting shadows.*
> **- James 1:17**

- **How does this passage affirm or inform your understanding of the goodness of God?**

_____

_____

_____

_____

What's God's Goodness Have to Do With Your Obedience?

Now that you have taken time to examine and better understand God's goodness, what difference can it make in your life? For one thing, your faith in God's goodness will tend to have a direct bearing on your obedience to Him. Consider the following multiple-choice question:

What's the connection between His goodness and the obedience of His people? *(Circle those that you think are true.)*

a. God only has authority in the lives of a select group for whom He shows His goodness and good intentions.

b. Your lack of faith in God's goodness causes you to resist giving God full authority in your life.

c. God's goodness to you depends on your faith in Christ.

d. You must demonstrate service to others before God will be good to you.

(See next page for answer.)

Answer: b

The answer is (b). Why is that? Take a look at answers a, c and d. Note why you think each of those answers involves a false view of God's goodness:

a. _____

c. _____

d. _____

You may have probably noticed through this exercise that it is common for people to think that God's goodness is conditional. Thinking of God's goodness as conditional often leads to insecurity. Thoughts like this tend to arise: "I'm not sure I've done enough for God to be good to me."

Doubting God's goodness has significant implications. When you doubt God's goodness, you will naturally be hesitant to submit to His authority. On the other hand, knowing and trusting in His goodness will foster submission and obedience.

But even when you begin to live obediently by God's power and grace, you face another concern. It can become very tempting to think that your obedience is what keeps God being good to you. Your obedience, however, never causes God to continue being good to you. He is not good to you because you obey.

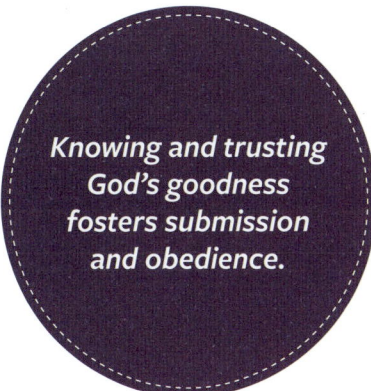

Knowing and trusting God's goodness fosters submission and obedience.

His goodness is a matter of grace; it's not earned by your works.

God's goodness is grounded in His character, not our performance. Some obey in fear because they believe God's love is conditional. We should obey in gratitude because we know God's love is unconditional.

Whenever you get that mixed up, you will have false expectations of God's goodness.

How Can You Trust God's Goodness When Life is Hard?

After all this, you might still be reluctant to fully trust that God is good. Your reasons might seem entirely justified if you have experienced lots of difficulties and trials in life. Past pain and suffering might cause you to doubt that God is good. No matter how many difficulties you have experienced, however, there is one certainty that can always remain as the supreme evidence of God's radical goodness—Jesus Christ.

Let's look for a moment at the life of a man who faced much adversity and difficulty, but who continued to know and trust in the God who is good.

Eric Liddell

A staggering truth is that you can find rest and peace in the midst of adversity. This seems like a dichotomy—how can you find rest in the midst of adversity? Whenever you see a tangible picture of this sort of thing, it is very striking.

One such example is found in the life of Eric Liddell. Some people know of him from the 1984 Academy Award-winning movie, Chariots of Fire, which portrayed Liddell winning a gold medal in the 1924 Olympics. What many people don't know is the rest of the story. He went on to be a missionary in China where he ended up in a Japanese concentration camp during WWII. One man who walked through those dark days with Eric wrote these things about him:

> He gave special care to the older people, the weak, and the ill, to whom the conditions in camp were very trying. Despite the squalor of the open cesspools, rats, flies and disease in the crowded camp, life took on a very normal routine, though without the faithful and cheerful support of Eric Liddell, many people would never have been able to manage.
>
> What was his secret? He unreservedly committed his life to Jesus Christ as his Saviour and Lord. That friendship meant everything to him. By the flickering light of a peanut-oil lamp early each morning he and a roommate in the men's cramped dormitory studied the Bible and talked with God for an hour every day.[4]

> *Look at a man in the midst of doubt and danger, and you will learn in his hour of adversity what he really is.[3]*
> **—Lucretius, ancient Roman philosopher**

While the quote from Lucretius points out that adversity reveals the character of a person, the Bible teaches how to develop the character of a person who can rest in adversity. God's Word teaches you how that's possible, and Eric Liddell had learned it was possible because of his commitment and submission to the friendship and

---

[3] Ed. Jason L. Saunders, Greek and Roman Philosophy After Aristotle, 1994. P31.
[4] http://www.ericliddell.org/ericliddell/recollections-by-people-who-knew-him/dr-david-j-mitchell ("Recollections of Eric Liddell," Dr. David J. Mitchell, Accessed Dec 1, 2016.)

lordship of Christ. Even though Liddell died of a brain tumor weeks before the war ended, God is still good.

Inspired by the example of Eric Liddell, let's return to a verse mentioned in the video. Reflect deeply on the verse below and then respond to the questions.

> *He who did not spare his own Son, but gave him up for us all—how will he not also, along with him, graciously give us all things?*
> **- Romans 8:32**

- **Describe in your own words how Jesus' life, death, and resurrection demonstrate God's goodness to you.**

- **What do you think is meant by the phrase "graciously give us all things"?**

> ***Natural blessings*** *include things like: beneficial opportunities (job offer, college acceptance), relationships (friendships, a boss, neighbors), natural beauty in nature, provision for life (food, housing, etc.)*
>
> ***Specific deliverances*** *include being rescued from: a difficult situation, an enemy or opponent, disease or illness, a potential accident or natural disaster*

- How have you experienced God graciously giving you good gifts in the past, whether "natural blessings" or "specific deliverances"?

_____

_____

_____

After studying these verses, hopefully you notice that God is not only good, but extravagantly good? His generosity knows no bounds. If He gave His Son, He is obviously willing and able to give you the very best—that which is for your greatest good.

The Fear of Missing Out and God's Goodness

If nothing else, we learn from the redeeming work of Jesus Christ that God is generous in His goodness. Nonetheless, we all experience moments when we still think we know better than God what is for our best. As a result, you will find that you struggle with idols. Everyone has them. For Chip, his idols were a relationship and basketball. You might find yourself thinking, "What if I'll miss out by not doing it?" When this happens, recall this passage:

> *For the LORD God is a sun and shield; the LORD bestows favor and honor; no good thing does he withhold from those whose walk is blameless.*
> - **Psalm 84:11**

The fear of missing out can be a strong drive, especially when we are tempted by all the world promises.

Before concluding our study of God's goodness, let's take some time to evaluate your own struggles with idols and then identify some concrete action steps you can take this week to claim God's promise that you will never miss out on any good thing when you walk by faith in Christ.

On the next page first make a list of some of the things you most fear missing out on if you fully surrender all areas of your life to God.

Next, come up with one thing you can do this week to surrender your life to God and trust in His goodness when faced with the temptations of that idol.

I have a fear of missing out because of this lie I have believed…	What I'm going to do this week when I'm tempted by that idol.
Example: *My reputation is my idol. I just want to be well-liked by everyone at the office. I fear that if I trust God to speak up when something is wrong that I won't be able to keep up my image as a likeable team player.*	*I'm going to trust that God will give me the strength to object when I see that we are mistreating a customer. I'll put Psalm 84:11 on my car dashboard to help me remember that God will not withhold His goodness from me even when I risk stirring up the pot by raising concerns at work.*

Putting Your Response to God in Prayer

This is the good part! Don't miss out by skipping this important step. Psalm 84:11 is a powerful promise! It can give you a great assurance that you will never miss out on any good thing. Take some time now to write down 10-12 ways God has been good to you in the last week and then thank Him for His goodness in prayer.

CHAPTER **TWO**

CHAPTER **THREE**
Sovereignty of God

All the peoples of the earth are regarded as nothing. He does as he pleases with the powers of heaven and the peoples of the earth. No one can hold back his hand or say to him: "What have you done?"

Daniel 4:35

CHAPTER **THREE**

BIG PICTURE

A Universal Truth

Control—everyone wants it at some level. Even when dealing with completely random events, like rolling dice, people try to grasp control. Studies have actually shown that people in casinos tend to throw dice harder if they want high numbers and softer for low numbers.[1] Regardless, the dice roll randomly.

In 1965, two researchers conducted an experiment that was designed to see how many decibels of sound a person could endure, or so the subjects were led to believe. They put one group of subjects into a room with blank walls and subjects from another group into a room that had a large "Panic" button on the wall. The button did nothing. It was just a prop.[2]

What happened? The subjects in the room with the panic button were able to withstand much more sound volume than those in the blank room. Why? Because they believed that they were in control. In psychology, this phenomenon has come be known as "the Illusion of control."

Sometimes people have more than an illusion of control. They have real power and influence. One U.S. president wanted so much control over his re-election campaign that he resorted to illegal spying on his opponent. He did so even when leading in the polls and with no significant threat of losing.

That was, in fact, only the tip of the iceberg of Nixon's desire for control. He spied on his own cabinet and staff. He ordered secret service officers to tail a senator. He wiretapped journalists. The desire to know what both your friends and enemies are saying can provide significant advantages.

In the end, Nixon could not control things near as much as he desired or hoped. His obsession to control ended up costing him the office.

Whether it is based on an illusion or not, human attempts to control their world are often a recipe for tragedy.

---

1 James M. Henslin, "Craps and Magic," American Journal of Sociology 73 (1967), P316. Cited in Michael Dorff, Indispensable and Other Myths: Why the CEO Pay Experiment Failed and How to Fix It, 2014. P180.

2 Rolf Dobelli, The Art of Thinking Clearly, 2013. P50.

CHAPTER THREE

Striving to Be in Control

Human attempts to control are not limited to the potentially tragic. Some people are controlling in the way they manicure their lawn or manage their Facebook page—surely not you, but those other people, right? The list of ways people try to control life goes on and on. But in the end, you and I have to realize we will never really be in complete control. It will never happen.

What about you? What kinds of things do you find yourself obsessing to control? *(Circle all that apply and add some of your own.)*

Diet	Personal health & fitness	Reputation in your community
Fantasy sports	Job performance	Photo albums
Presentation of your home	Body shape	Daughter's wedding
Behavior of your kids	Social media	Finances
School grades	Career path	Retirement plans

Other: _____

Other: _____

If we're honest with ourselves, we have a hard enough time controlling some elements of our own lives... we certainly do not get it right all of the time. In our human experience, even our best efforts are not as reliable as a Swiss watch. Now, with all of the struggles we face for control, imagine for a moment what it means to be in control of the course of 8 billion lives, not the mention the rest of the natural world in the universe. That's awesome. And that's God's sovereignty.

CHAPTER THREE

> **Watch Chip Ingram's Teaching and fill in the notes below.**
>
> ▶ **Sovereignty of God**

"When we say God is sovereign, we declare that by virtue of his creatorship over all life and reality, His all-knowing, all-powerful, and benevolent rule, that He is in fact the Lord of all Lords, King of all Kings, and in absolute control of time and eternity. Nothing will come into my life today that He did not either allow or decree for my ultimate good."[3]
- Chip Ingram, The Real God

How Does God Reveal His Sovereignty to Us?

Through His _____

Through His _____

Through _____

Through _____

    His supernatural _____

    His _____

    His _____

    His willful _____ & _____

    His _____

Through redeeming the _____ in our lives.

    The _____ principle.

---

[3] See Real God, Chp5.

CHAPTER THREE

Two Questions the Sovereignty of God Raises

1. If God is sovereign, why did/does He _____ evil, pain, and suffering? (Recommended reading: *The Problem of Pain*, C.S. Lewis)

2. If God is sovereign over all people and events in history, doesn't this make a sham of _____? (Recommended reading: *Chosen but Free*, Norman Geisler)

How Must We Respond to a Sovereign God?

_____ before the King of the universe. *Philippians 2:9-11*

_____ all that comes into your life is either allowed or decreed by a good God who will use it for your benefit. *Romans 8:28-29; Genesis 50:20*

_____ in awe the mystery and majesty of His kind, compassionate, just, and sovereign rule of all that is or will ever be. *Romans 11:33-36*

Application = _____ **God for who He is, not merely for what He has done.**

The Sovereignty of God

The following questions will help you reflect on what you watched on the video. If you are in a group spend some time sharing with others.

1. In Genesis 50:20 Joseph said, *"You intended to harm me, but God intended it for good to accomplish what is now being done, the saving of many lives."* As you reflect back over your life, what is something that was painful, bad, and maybe even evil that God in His sovereignty used for good?

2. Read Colossians 1:15-18. In light of the supremacy and sovereignty of Christ, what phrase most stands out to you? Why?

3. Read Daniel 4:34-35 and Romans 11:33-36. How should God's sovereignty impact your worship?

4. Romans 8:28-29 says, *"And we know that God causes everything to work together for the good of those who love God and are called according to his purpose for them. For God knew his people in advance, and he chose them to become like his Son, so that his Son would be the firstborn among many brothers and sisters."* How can God's sovereignty bring comfort?

5. In light of your current personal circumstances, how should the truth of God's sovereignty impact your perspective, attitude, and words?

6. If you had a friend who was confused by conflicting ideas of God's sovereignty and man's free will, what would you say to them?

As you conclude your group time, spend a few minutes praying together. But, before you pray, take a few moments to answer the following question. How should God's sovereignty impact how we pray?

Now, pray together. Thank God for his sovereignty and if there is some area of your life that you need to submit to God's sovereignty, do so in prayer.

God's Sovereignty Portrayed in His Promises

This next section is for you to complete on your own. Take what you have learned and turn it into action.

God is in control—complete control. Seems pretty simple, right? Nothing surprises Him; nothing confuses Him.

Fine, but what difference does it make in my world and in my life?

As you turn your attention to several promises made in the Bible, you'll realize that the kind of control that God has is not something like poise or self-control. It is absolute control of all things.

Promises express a person's intentions. From a human perspective, you learn to trust a person's promise only when you trust that person's honesty and ability to fulfill the promise.

To start with, let's look at how God's promises communicate intention. In particular, what does God promise and what do we learn about His sovereignty from His promises?

There are many promises that God makes in the Bible; let's look at just two. Turn your attention to two of the most important and dramatic promises that God has ever made.

CHAPTER THREE

PROMISE 1: Christ's Supremacy

We'll start by looking at a promise that all will eventually recognize Christ's supremacy

> *Therefore God exalted him to the highest place and gave him the name that is above every name, that at the name of Jesus every knee should bow, in heaven and on earth and under the earth, and every tongue confess that Jesus Christ is Lord, to the glory of God the Father.*
> **-Philippians 2:9-11**

In Romans 14, you can find another expression of this promise that is more explicit about a future moment when all people will acknowledge God's sovereignty:

> *For we will all stand before God's judgment seat. It is written: "'As surely as I live,' says the Lord, 'every knee will bow before me; every tongue will confess to God.'" So then, each of us will give an account of himself to God.*
> **-Romans 14: 10-12**

Let's turn to a few questions that help think through what this promise was meant to communicate to the original audience and what it means for us today.

Why might the promise of Christ's supremacy (Phil. 2:9-11, Romans 14:10-12) have been important for a group of minority Christians in the first century world of the Roman Empire? *(Mark all that apply)*

○ To know that their unjust persecution under Roman authorities would be held to account

○ To know that their Lord Jesus Christ would some day reign with justice

○ To remember that they are personally accountable to Him

○ To remember that they owe their allegiance and worship to Him

If you marked all four, you're right. The promise that all will eventually bow to Christ communicated to them that their persecutors were not ultimately sovereign. This promise assured those Christians in the Roman Empire there is only one sovereign Lord—all are accountable to Him. He is the Lord, not the emperor.

So what about you? What does it mean for your life knowing that Christ is sovereign and will one day make everything right?

Ask yourself this question:

How does the promise of Christ's supremacy affect my emotions and thoughts, my attitude and actions? *(Mark all that apply)*

- ○ It gives me hope to know that a just and righteous Lord will someday reign. Under His reign, there will be no war, no crime, no racism, and no abuse of the environment.

- ○ It helps me control my anger since all the injustice I experience will ultimately be held to account.

- ○ It challenges me to cultivate an attitude of quiet confidence in the face of uncertain or unstable national and world affairs—a confidence that comes from the security I feel in my relationship with Christ.

- ○ It humbles me to think about how amazing it is that I've been redeemed by the same Lord who could justly condemn me.

Surely you can relate to some of these more than others and you could add many to this list. There are many ways God's sovereignty can be an encouragement to us. However, you might also come away thinking:

Fine, I know that Jesus will come out on top in the end and I have comfort that I'll be on His team. But, what about now? Is He really in control of this messed up world? It certainly doesn't seem that way.

PROMISE 2: God Works for the Good of All Who Love Him

In light of those concerns, take a look at this promise:

> *And we know that in all things God works for the good of those who love him, who have been called according to his purpose.*
> **- Romans 8:28**

While the first promise provides a great deal of assurance for those who place their faith in Christ, this promise might leave you scratching your head at best, or angry at worst.
How is this promise possible when so much bad happens to people? How is it for the good of people who love God to experience tragedy? How can it be good, for

example, when a godly woman of three young children is diagnosed with cancer and dies shortly afterward? How is it good for her children or her God-fearing husband?

In the face of such tragedies, we must lean with all our might into the promise of Romans 8:28. Take some time to think about some of the most painful or tragic circumstances of your own life or the lives of those close to you. Reflect on and take notes on how you would respond to the following question in light of those difficult experiences:

- **How have I seen God working "for the good of those who love him" in a painful or tragic circumstance?**

_____

_____

_____

_____

Now let's review for a second. God has communicated His intentions through promises. Those promises express radical supremacy and also a radical commitment for the good of those who love Him.

- God promises to bring all to submission under Christ's authority, both those who lovingly submit and those who rebel. That's a radical claim of ultimate sovereignty.

- God will take care of those who love Him in the meantime. God works good in the lives of His own, even in a messed-up, pain-filled, sinful world. That's an amazing claim.

God's Sovereignty Proven in the Work of Christ

Promises communicate intentions, but good intentions are cheap. Aren't they? Without a doubt, you know this all too well from life experience. The Bible makes some radical promises, but how do you know that God can deliver on those promises?

The answer is Jesus. But that begs another question. How is it that Jesus can convince you that God is sovereign and delivers on His promises? We could look at Jesus' conception and birth for examples of God fulfilling promises (Isaiah 7:13-14 and Luke 1:26-37). We could also look at examples from Jesus' life and ministry (Isaiah 42:7-6 and John 9). For sake of time, we will look only at an example of God's promise keeping in the death and resurrection of Christ. It is the most astounding display of God's promise-keeping and sovereignty that the world has ever witnessed.

Jesus' Death and Resurrection

There are many examples of how the details of Jesus' trial and crucifixion fulfilled prophecies. However, we're going to look at just one Messianic promise from Isaiah to see how Jesus fulfills a promise while also demonstrating God's sovereignty.

> *After the suffering of his soul, he will see the light [of life] and be satisfied; by his knowledge my righteous servant will justify many, and he will bear their iniquities. Therefore I will give him a portion among the great, and he will divide the spoils with the strong, because he poured out his life unto death, and was numbered with the transgressors. For he bore the sin of many, and made intercession for the transgressors.*
> - **Isaiah 53:11-12**

Now look at two excerpts from the gospels in which Jesus is foretelling of His death and resurrection.

> *"We are going up to Jerusalem," [Jesus] said, "and the Son of Man will be betrayed to the chief priests and teachers of the law. They will condemn him to death and will hand him over to the Gentiles, who will mock him and spit on him, flog him and kill him. Three days later He will rise...*
> *For even the Son of Man did not come to be served, but to serve, and to give his life as a ransom for many."*
> - **Mark 10:33-34, 45**

> *"The reason my Father loves me is that I lay down my life—only to take it up again. No one takes it from me, but I lay it down of my own accord. I have authority to lay it down and authority to take it up again. This command I received from my Father."*
> - **John 10:17-18 (Jesus speaking)**

Let's stop for a moment and reflect deeply on these verses.

- **How do the verses in Mark and John demonstrate the fulfillment of the promise in Isaiah 53?**

_____
_____
_____
_____

No single event from Jesus' birth, life, crucifixion, or resurrection provides a complete picture of God revealing His sovereignty. However, looking at the whole picture presents a striking picture of a God who has worked out the events of human history to fulfill His promises. The climax of those promises is found in the Messiah. As was promised to Abraham many centuries before, God would bless all nations of the earth through the Messiah (Genesis 22:15-18). And God was able and willing to fulfill that promise, demonstrating His sovereignty.

Living Under God's Sovereignty

Now it's time to get practical. What difference does all of this make for our daily lives? Three ways: Surrender, Refusing to Worry, and Worship.

RESPONSE #1: *Surrender to God's Sovereignty*

Let's look back at Philippians 2:9-11.

> *Therefore God exalted him to the highest place and gave him the name that is above every name, that at the name of Jesus every knee should bow, in heaven and on earth and under the earth, and every tongue confess that Jesus Christ is Lord, to the glory of God the Father.*
> - **Philippians 2:9-11**

While it is a general declaration of Christ's sovereignty, it has personal implications. Each of us must bow in absolute surrender to our personal Lord.

What does that look like in your life? It means you need to look at the areas of your life where you have a pattern of clinging to control.

Look back at what you identified at the beginning of this chapter (page 36) to the areas you most seek to control in your life. Below, copy the top three areas you seek to control in your life into the left column of chart. Then in the right-hand column write out some steps you can take this week to release control of those areas to the lordship of Christ. There's an example provided to help you to generate ideas.

My top three control obsessions	What I'll do this week to submit this obsession to the lordship of Christ.
Example: Make sure my kids are always well behaved.	- Take opportunities to praise them rather than always correcting. - Allow them to go to their cousins' house without me. - Pray for them to increasingly submit to the lordship of Christ as they grow older and for me to release them to Him

CHAPTER THREE

RESPONSE #2: *Refuse to Worry*

One of the great ironies is that the areas of life we try most to control often are the sources of greatest worry. They are not, however, the only sources of worry. Things very much outside of our control are also sources of worry, like waiting for the results of a medical test. It's important to remember that every moment you worry is wasted time. No amount of worrying ever changed an outcome.

What are a two or three things you are worrying about right now?

_____
_____
_____
_____
_____

Worrying is concentrating more on fear than on God. Read Philippians 4:6-8 and then write a prayer here asking God to release you from worry as you reflect on His sovereignty.

_____
_____
_____
_____
_____

RESPONSE #3: *Worship God*

Select one of the three options below or one of your own as an expression of worship this week:

- Share with a friend how God's sovereignty has helped assure you in a time of difficulty.

    Name of friend: _____

- Sort through your favorite collection of worship songs and select a song about God's sovereignty to listen to and reflect on throughout the week.

    Song Titles: _____

    _____

    _____

- Write out a list of all the things you are most concerned about in life. At the bottom of your list, write in all capital letters: GOD IS IN CONTROL, then pray and ask God to help you to rest in His sovereignty.

    Concerns: _____

    _____

    _____

    _____

    _____

    _____

    _____

CHAPTER **FOUR**
Holiness of God

Holy, holy, holy is the Lord Almighty;
the whole earth is full of his glory.

Isaiah 6:3

Making Sense of Holiness

Write the first 5 words that come to your mind when you think of the word "holy." (Force yourself to quickly respond without thinking about it too much.)

1. _____

2. _____

3. _____

4. _____

5. _____

Hallowed Ground

Have you ever entered a place that has special meaning to you—a **hallowed*** place—and you just sensed it. Maybe you stopped breathing for a moment or you just stood staring, taking it all in. Depending on your interests, it could be a variety of places: Arlington National Cemetery for a veteran, Carnegie Hall for a music lover, Gettysburg for a history buff, Wrigley Field for a baseball fan, the Louvre for an art student, Wimbledon for a tennis player. Those are hallowed places.

While we don't always make the connection in our minds, when we treat a place as hallowed we are treating it as holy. That place is different. It's the opposite of an ordinary place. Moses was told by God at the burning bush that he was standing on holy ground, and it certainly was holy. It was holy because God was present in a unique way at that moment.

However, we naturally tend to treat not only places but other sorts of things as holy or hallowed. If you have a signed jersey from your favorite athlete what do you do with it? You put it in a special frame and hang it in a special place. You don't wear it or throw it in the wash with your ordinary clothes. Or what about that special memory you shared with a loved one. You don't share that lightly or with random strangers. You cherish it as a special moment in your past.

Hallowed, adj.   Something revered as holy

CHAPTER **FOUR**

> **How do most people describe holiness?**
>
> If you feel overwhelmed by the concept of holiness, you're not alone. In a recent national study, when people were asked to describe what it means to be holy, the most common answer was, "I don't know."¹

No One is Like Him

Remember back at the beginning of this study of God's attributes, when we spoke of awe? There may be nothing more awe-inspiring than God's holiness. Moses sung of His holiness after God parted the waters of the Red Sea and the Hebrews passed through escaping the Egyptians:

> *"Who is like you—majestic in holiness, awesome in glory, working wonders?"*
> - **Exodus 15:11**

It's a rhetorical question; the answer reveals a part of the essence of holiness—"No one is like Him."

Moses points out that God's holiness is majestic. Majesty is related to words like beauty, dignity, and splendor. God's holiness also involves His moral purity. His moral perfection is different than anything we experience in our fallen world. In fact, it's no exaggeration to say that God is holy in all His attributes. He is unique in His goodness. No one is good like God. He is also holy in His sovereignty, in His wisdom, and so on.

Those sentences might make your mind spin a bit. The concept of God's holiness can be difficult for us because it speaks to what is so different from who we are.

If God is overwhelmingly majestic and morally pure, how can we who are so much less know Him at all?

Yet as we have already discovered, God commands us to seek Him with all our hearts and delights in revealing Himself in ways we can understand. To be sure, when it comes to understanding the holiness of an almighty God, we have our work cut out for us. We may never fully understand His holiness but we can learn something about the holiness of God, and what we learn can transform our lives in the most profound ways.

Now let's turn to the video to examine this challenging attribute of God. Like many who have sought to see and know God, you just might be brought to your knees.

---

1 "The Concept of Holiness Baffles Most Americans." Barna.com. Feb. 20, 2006.

CHAPTER **FOUR**

> **VIDEO** — Watch Chip Ingram's Teaching and fill in the notes below.
>
> ▶ **The Holiness of God**

"We know nothing like the divine holiness. It stands apart, unique, unapproachable, incomprehensible and unattainable. The natural man is blind to it. He may fear God's power and admire His wisdom, but His holiness he cannot even imagine."[2]
- A.W. Tozer, Knowledge of the Holy

How Does God Reveal His Holiness to Us?

Through _____ _____ *Exodus 3; Isaiah 6*

Through _____

Through _____ _____ *Exodus 20; Leviticus & Deuteronomy*

Through the _____

Through His _____ & _____ *Joshua 7; Acts 5; Nehemiah 1; 1 Corinthians 11*

Through His _____
- a holy life   *John 8:46*
- an unholy death   *2 Corinthians 5:21*
- a holy resurrection   *John 20:26-31*
- a holy priesthood   *Hebrews 9: 11-28*

Through His _____ *Isaiah 6:1-6; 1 Corinthians 6:18-20*

---

[2] AW Tozer, Knowledge of the Holy, 1961. P104.

God's Holiness Raises Two Important Questions

If God is so holy that he cannot even gaze at sin, how can sinful people like us have a relationship with Him?

If trusting in Christ's work on the cross blots out our sin before God and we are holy in His sight, why do we keep on sinning?

- _____: positional holiness (our position with God)

- _____: progressive holiness (making progress)

- _____: permanently holy (like Him)

How Must We Respond to the Holiness of God?

It's a _____ we make.. *Hebrews 12:14*

It's a _____ we obey. *1 Peter 13-16; Hebrews 13:4*

The Holiness of God

The following questions will help you reflect on what you watched on the video. If you are in a group spend some time sharing with others.

1. The call to holiness is demanding and yet, it is also the path to God's very best for our lives. When you hear Peter's command to be holy just like God is holy, what comes to your mind? And, what are the practical implications of that command? Where do you struggle most?

2. When the average person in our generation hears the word "holiness", what kinds of thoughts and images come to their mind?

3. In Isaiah 6:1-7 the prophet encounters the holiness of God. From this passage, what most stands out to you about God's holiness? Why?

4. Chip said, "We live in the day where the holiness of God has been neglected and we have a low view of God." Why do you think this is the case and what can we do to correct this problem?

5. Hebrews 12:14 NIV says, "Make every effort to live in peace with all men and to be holy; without holiness no one will see the Lord." What does the writer mean when he says, "without holiness no one will see the Lord?"

6. Read 1 Corinthians 6:18-20. What does this passage teach us about personal holiness?

Begin your prayer time by reading Isaiah 40:18-26. And, let this passage guide your time of prayer. Spend time thanking God for his majesty and holiness. Then, spend a few minutes praying for each other and your pursuit of personal holiness.

God's Holiness Revealed

This next section is for you to complete on your own. Take what you have learned and turn it into action.

The Burning Bush

We have already spoken about Moses several times in our quest to know the real God, and that's no surprise. Of all the individuals portrayed in the Bible, Moses certainly had one of the most intimate relationships with God. In studying God's holiness, Moses' story is an obvious choice to help expand our understanding.

We'll begin by looking at Moses' first encounter with God.

Before you read it, what do you expect will be Moses' response during his very first encounter with the God of his fathers? *Pick one from below.*

○ He asked God to show him His face.

○ He bowed down in reverence.

○ He worshiped him.

○ He was terrified and hid his face.

Now, read the following excerpt from **Exodus 3**. Do it quickly. Like you would a story.

3 Now Moses was tending the flock of Jethro his father-in-law, the priest of Midian, and he led the flock to the far side of the wilderness and came to Horeb, the mountain of God. 2 There the angel of the Lord appeared to him in flames of fire from within a bush. Moses saw that though the bush was on fire it did not burn up. 3 So Moses thought, "I will go over and see this strange sight—why the bush does not burn up."

4 When the Lord saw that he had gone over to look, God called to him from within the bush, "Moses! Moses!"

And Moses said, "Here I am."

5 "Do not come any closer," God said. "Take off your sandals, for the place where you are standing is holy ground." 6 Then he said, "I am the God of your father, the God of Abraham, the God of Isaac and the God of Jacob." At this, Moses hid his face, because he was afraid to look at God.

7 The Lord said, "I have indeed seen the misery of my people in Egypt. I have heard them crying out because of their slave drivers, and I am concerned about their suffering. 8 So I have come down to rescue them from the hand of the Egyptians and to bring them up out of that land into a good and spacious land, a land flowing with milk and honey—the home of the Canaanites, Hittites, Amorites, Perizzites, Hivites and Jebusites. 9 And now the cry of the Israelites has reached me, and I have seen the way the Egyptians are oppressing them. 10 So now, go. I am sending you to Pharaoh to bring my people the Israelites out of Egypt."

11 But Moses said to God, "Who am I that I should go to Pharaoh and bring the Israelites out of Egypt?"

12 And God said, "I will be with you. And this will be the sign to you that it is I who have sent you: When you have brought the people out of Egypt, you will worship God on this mountain.

13 Moses said to God, "Suppose I go to the Israelites and say to them, 'The God of your fathers has sent me to you,' and they ask me, 'What is his name?' Then what shall I tell them?"

14 God said to Moses, "I am who I am. This is what you are to say to the Israelites: 'I am has sent me to you.'"

Now, let's dig into this a bit more. Go back and read the passage again, this time go slowly. You might even want to read it out loud. Then read it a third time and circle or underline all of the key words.

After you have read the passage three times, brainstorm as many observations of God's holiness as you can from this passage. Refer to the two points on the right that describe God's holiness.

Verse: _____

Observation: _____

_____

Verse: _____

Observation: _____
_____

Verse: _____

Observation: _____
_____

Verse: _____

Observation: _____
_____

Verse: _____

Observation: _____
_____

Verse: _____

Observation: _____
_____

Now that you have taken some time in the passage, let's consider a few takeaways. One thing you probably noticed is that being in God's presence is nothing to take lightly. Thus, when we approach God, whether in prayer as a family before dinner or when reading God's word in Scripture, proper respect is due. His holiness demands a profound reverence on our part. But, also notice that God moves toward Moses. God interacts with Moses in spite of the great disparity between who God is and who Moses is. God wants to move toward you too. Be prepared to welcome that, but never lose reverence for your holy God.

God's Name

One of the most striking things about Exodus 3 is the name God reveals to Moses. Perhaps more than anything God's name Yahweh reveals his holiness. This Hebrew word literally means "I am." Thus, Yahweh is not just one unique being among other beings. He is not just powerful or all-knowing. He is the source of all existence. He is self-existing and all that exists owes its existence to Him. What is extraordinary is that this magnificent One is now, in the story of Moses, preparing to have a new kind of relationship with a group of people who will represent Him in their world.

A New Boss

Imagine that you have taken a new job and you quickly discover that your boss has two qualities that stand out. Your boss is (1) absolutely committed to your professional development and (2) expects the highest standards of performance and integrity.

How do you think you would respond in this situation? *(Mark all that apply)*

- ○ Seek the advice of my boss often
- ○ Try to get reassigned as soon as possible
- ○ Try to emulate my boss
- ○ Be worried about my performance
- ○ Struggle with a lack of motivation
- ○ Do whatever I could to please my boss
- ○ Listen carefully to my boss' instructions and expectations

Moses and the Hebrews in the book of Exodus find themselves in a similar situation. While they have lived under a cruel and unjust boss, Pharaoh, a new "boss" has come on the scene—or rather their original, rightful master. Only in this case, it's not the kind of boss you might expect to have in a new job. He is altogether different. He is unwaveringly committed to their good (Exodus 19: 5-6, also refer to chapter two). He desires for them to be His "treasured possession."

God wants them to be His people. But in order to be His people they will have to adopt His standards. And that's no small task—to say the least.

New Commands for a Holy Nation

Through the agency of Moses, God delivers the Hebrews from slavery. After releasing them from Egypt, God begins a process of forging them into a new nation. They will not be like the other nations. He's going to give them thorough instructions so they will understand what He expects from them. He's going to give them the Ten

Commandments as well as the Law—that long set of instructions for how to live. God sums up his expectations with the following statement:

> *I am the LORD who brought you up out of Egypt to be your God; therefore be holy, because I am holy.*
> **- Leviticus 11:45**

Let's take a look at one particular command in the Law to get a glimpse of what this was to look like in the Hebrews' lives.

> *Remember the Sabbath day by keeping it holy. Six days you shall labor and do all your work, but the seventh day is a Sabbath to the LORD your God. On it you shall not do any work, neither you, nor your son or daughter, nor your manservant or maidservant, nor your animals, nor the alien within your gates. For in six days the LORD made the heavens and the earth, the sea, and all that is in them, but he rested on the seventh day. Therefore the LORD blessed the Sabbath day and made it holy.*
>
> *Six days do your work, but on the seventh day do not work, so that your ox and your donkey may rest and the slave born in your household, and the alien as well, may be refreshed.*
> **- Exodus 20:8-11, 23:12**

> *But for the sake of my name I did what would keep it from being profaned in the eyes of the nations they lived among and in whose sight I had revealed myself to the Israelites by bringing them out of Egypt. Therefore I led them out of Egypt and brought them into the desert. I gave them my decrees and made known to them my laws, for the man who obeys them will live by them. Also I gave them my Sabbaths as a sign between us, so they would know that I the LORD made them holy.*
> **- Ezekiel 20: 9-12**

As you review these verses, circle or underline the benefits that are promised for the Hebrews if they live holy lives, obeying the Law and keeping the Sabbath.

Notice from the Exodus and Ezekiel passage, there are at least three expressed purposes of the Law and in particular the Sabbath:

- The Law gave health and preservation for those who lived by them (including rest and refreshment in the case of the Sabbath).
- The Law set the Hebrews apart from the nations among whom they lived and honored the true God.
- The Law reminded and assured the Hebrews that they belonged to God.

God not only saved the Hebrews from slavery in Egypt, He set them up for success as a nation—a nation intended to be holy representatives of Yahweh.

A Holy Messiah for an Unholy People

As you probably know, time and again the Hebrews failed to remain faithful to God and His commands. They were not holy as He commanded them to be. The Old Testament is filled with examples. They often took on the unholy practices of neighboring nations, forsaking God's calling to be different. In spite of their regular failures, God's prophets spoke of an ultimate solution. A savior, the Messiah, was promised. And it turns out, this Messiah and His mission are all about holiness. While the Hebrews were unable to live holy lives, their Messiah was able to live a holy life and make holy those who trust in Him:

> *Therefore he is able to save completely those who come to God through him, because he always lives to intercede for them. Such a high priest meets our need—one who is holy, blameless, pure, set apart from sinners, exalted above the heavens.*
> **- Hebrews 7: 25-26**

Of course this high priest-messiah is the Lord Jesus Christ, whose life was untainted by immorality—He was holy in his righteousness. As we see in 2 Peter 1:1, we receive saving faith "through the righteousness of our God and Savior Jesus Christ."

Because of Christ's righteousness, He was worthy to bear the punishment of our sin. As the prophet wrote in anticipation of the Messiah's coming:

> *He was pierced for our transgressions, he was crushed for our iniquities; the punishment that brought us peace was upon him, and by his wounds we are healed.*
> **- Isaiah 53:5**

Since most of us are not Jewish, it's great news that the salvation offered by the long-awaited Messiah applies to all people (see Romans 10:12). This new group of redeemed people—the Church—was purchased by God and for relationship with Him. Followers of Christ are called to be a different kind of people and to live different kinds of lives. We are called, in short, to be holy. Notice how the command to be holy, previously given to the Hebrews, is now repeated for all who are God's people through faith in Christ:

> *But just as he who called you is holy, so be holy in all you do; for it is written: "Be holy, because I am holy."*
> **- 1 Peter 1:15-16**

The obvious question at this point is:

How does this group of Christ-followers—the Church—have hope of being holy any more than the Hebrews did?

The answer to this question, again, has everything to do with God and His holiness.

God's holiness in the gift of the Spirit

In the days preceding Jesus' trial, crucifixion, and resurrection, He began to speak about something mysterious. A "helper" was going to come to His disciples in the wake of His leaving. The helper was none other than the third person of the Trinity—the Holy Spirit.

> *The Counselor, the Holy Spirit, whom the Father will send in my name, will teach you all things and will remind you of everything I have said to you.*
> **- John 14:26**

> *But you will receive power when the Holy Spirit comes on you.*
> **- Acts 1:8**

Acts 2 describes the dramatic coming of the Holy Spirit, now known as Pentecost. Not surprisingly, the lives of the disciples are radically changed as a result. The Holy Spirit comes to help make holy those He inhabits. Emphasizing how holy this new people of God are to be, Paul asks the Corinthians this rhetorical question:

> *Don't you know that you yourselves are God's temple and that God's Spirit lives in you?*
> **- 1 Corinthians 3:16**

Can you hear the urgency and intensity in Paul's question? In the video, Chip too made much of this. And rightly so. Knowing that God's Holy Spirit inhabits your life should make a massive difference in how you approach life.

If you have received salvation in Christ, His Spirit now dwells in you and is working to help make you holy. Take some time and reflect on ways that the Holy Spirit's indwelling impacts you.

When you stop to consider that God's Holy Spirit dwells in you—that you are a Temple of the Holy One—how does that impact your thoughts and feelings about your life circumstances?

_____

_____

_____

A church being made holy

The realization that you are a temple inhabited by God can have a powerful impact on your inner life—how you feel and think. And what's more, His Holy Spirit is doing a work in your life.

God's Spirit is working for a transformation of your inner life as well as how you live outwardly. But that transformation requires a partnership with you. Paul drives at our role in that partnership in Romans:

> *Therefore, I urge you, brothers, in view of God's mercy, to offer your bodies as living sacrifices, holy and pleasing to God--this is your spiritual act of worship. Do not conform any longer to the pattern of this world, but be transformed by the renewing of your mind.*
> **- Romans 12: 1-2**

With the Spirit's help we are to resist conforming to the world. If we conform, we are, by definition, not achieving a holy life. Conforming is to take on the same form—to be common with the world.

In the 1 John passage below, circle those phrases that identify characteristics of the world's pattern of living.

> *Do not love the world or anything in the world. If anyone loves the world, the love of the Father is not in him. For everything in the world--the cravings of sinful man, the lust of his eyes and the boasting of what he has and does--comes not from the Father but from the world.*
> **1 John 2:15-16**

You should have noticed that three general qualities are mentioned. Looking at those three qualities, assess your own life.

In what specific ways do you have difficulty resisting the pressure to conform to the world?

In my cravings: _____

In the lust of my eyes: _____

In my boasting of what I possess and have achieved: _____
_____

In the New Testament we see the theme of God's people living holy lives. There are many references to followers of Christ being in the world but not of the world. However, the point is not merely to avoid the world or resist the world, but to live in it so that the world can see Christ in us.

Notice how Paul explains in 1 Corinthians the different way that he and his fellow Christians have acted:

> *Our conscience testifies that we have conducted ourselves in the world, and especially in our relations with you, in the holiness and sincerity that are from God.*
> **- 1 Corinthians 1:12**

What <u>one thing</u> do you commit to do this week to be holy—separate and not conformed to the world—in partnership with and by the power of the Spirit who desires to see you mature in holiness? *(Consider your answers to the previous question as areas for growth here.)*

_____

_____

_____

Holy, holy, holy

God's holiness is a consistent theme woven through redemptive history. We see glimpses of His holiness in various events recorded in the Bible. We will more fully understand—and worship—His holiness when we stand before the throne of God.

In the book of Revelation, John is given a glimpse into that throne room. What we see reinforces the lessons we have learned about God's holiness and echoes the revelation of God's name to Moses:

> *Each of the four living creatures had six wings and was covered with eyes all around, even under his wings. Day and night they never stop saying: "Holy, holy, holy is the Lord God Almighty, who was, and is, and is to come…"*
>
> *"You are worthy, our Lord and God, to receive glory and honor and power, for you created all things, and by your will they were created and have their being."*
> **- Revelation 4:8, 11**

Notice the emphatic way that holiness is highlighted in the vision of God upon His throne. Even these creatures who are awe-inspiring themselves are in awe of God. It will be the same for us. Even after we have been fully transformed in glory at the end of time—a church made holy as the bride of a holy Messiah—we will still be in awe of God's holiness.

The great God of all creation, high above all things, is holy in a way that we can only just begin to understand here on earth. It will be an awe-inspiring experience when we are present with Him and the full holiness of God is revealed.

So who is like God? There is none like the great I AM.

Putting your response to God in prayer

Read the prayer below and if it reflects your heart, pray it to God. You can also personalize it in the space provided below.

O Lord God, holy and pure, awesome in majesty, as I consider Your perfection, grant that I might commit to holy ways, think holy thoughts, live in holy obedience, and reject evil with a holy attitude.

Let me hear the tender conviction of Your Spirit and help me remember that You are jealous for Your holiness. Because of Your love, You see the pain our sins will bring us, and You long to rescue us. So that Your name never be profaned in my life, You have my permission to do whatever You need to do to make me holy.
In Jesus' name, Amen.

CHAPTER FIVE
Wisdom of God

*Oh, the depth of the riches of the wisdom and knowledge of God!
How unsearchable his judgments, and his paths beyond tracing out!*

Romans 11:33

Unshakable Confidence

Roni, as she was called, served with her husband Jim as missionaries in the country of Peru.

After adopting a second child the entire family flew to the border near Brazil to obtain a permanent visa for little Charity. With mission accomplished they headed back to their village area in a small Cessna plane. They were about 40 minutes out from landing when something happened that forever changed the destiny of their family.

The Peruvian military mistakenly decided that this plane was carrying drugs. Without any radio communication from the Peruvian air force, the fighter jets opened fire on the small Cessna. More than 50 bullets penetrated the plane.

The plane began spiraled downward and crashed into the Amazon River. As the plane sank into the murky waters, Jim was able to pull Roni and little 7 month old Charity from the plane but he quickly discovered that they were both dead.

Here is an innocent 7 month old baby and a 35 year old woman who had sacrificed much to serve as a missionary in a difficult part of the world. If you allow yourself to linger very long over stories like this one, you find yourself asking some hard and uncomfortable questions.

It can make you question God's fairness, kindness, love, and power... and wisdom. How could that have been God's wise plan for Roni?

Part of our problem is that we have a limited, finite, foggy view of life and eternity. And usually God doesn't let us see the whole picture. But, sovereign and just and good and loving, He cannot help but be wise.

A few weeks before her death Roni wrote the following words in her journal.

"Life doesn't always give you a storybook ending. You do not always end up with the answer to your prayers that you desire. God often chooses to do something different with your life than you envisioned. But it's ok. He's still God, and He still loves you. As long as your confidence in God remains strong in the midst of all the questions and myriad of emotions you will be ok. He is the only one who remains constant, and life is good if you stay in His arms—God's loving arms. You may not understand where He leads, but you will be safe and secure with Him anywhere, even in death."

She had an unshakeable confidence that God was good, sovereign, loving and therefore... wise.

Why Wisdom Matters

When life confronts us with really challenging situations, our responses usually fall somewhere between two extremes. On the one hand there's hubris, and on the other hand there's hopelessness. Neither one of these options understands and honors the wisdom of God. Let's take a look at why.

Hubris

Hubris is defined as excessive pride or self-confidence. In ancient Greek plays, it was often the hubris of the hero that led to his downfall. Hubris looks at challenges and declares, "I've got this! I can solve this myself because I know exactly what to do."

We may believe we have the financial resources to weather any storm. We may believe we have the smarts and talent to solve any problem that may come our way at work. Or we may believe we have the experience and best practices to help us overcome any challenge with our families. We may even put our trust in our own spiritual maturity or our own "wisdom," rather than seeking out the wisdom of God. Hubris is confident it has everything it needs to overcome any challenge.

Hopelessness

While hubris responds to challenges with brazen confidence, hopelessness responds with the opposite. Hubris says "I know precisely what to do." Hopelessness says "I have no idea what to do."

For some of us, a sense of hopelessness comes after all our best-laid plans have fallen to ruin. Others have simply been beaten down by life, or have been trained to think that they will never succeed at anything. Faced with a challenge, they are paralyzed. And sometimes a problem just seems hopeless to begin with. When you don't know anything about finances, financial problems can immediately paralyze you. When you don't understand legal documents and can't afford a lawyer, a pending lawsuit can cause despair.

Look at the list below. When you face problems in these areas, do you lean more toward hubris, or more toward hopelessness?

	Hubris									*Hopelessness*
Marriage	1	2	3	4	5	6	7	8	9	10
Parenting	1	2	3	4	5	6	7	8	9	10
Finances	1	2	3	4	5	6	7	8	9	10
Work	1	2	3	4	5	6	7	8	9	10
Friendships	1	2	3	4	5	6	7	8	9	10

The Way of Wisdom

The way of wisdom leads neither to hubris nor to hopelessness. According to the Bible, both responses are flawed. And both point toward the need for God's wisdom.

When we feel hubris, we're ignoring all our limitations. There are so many things we don't know, don't control, and cannot do on our own. The Bible warns against trying to solve all our problems by our own strength, talents, and effort, with a lack of faith or reliance upon God.

There's a sense in which hopelessness is closer to the truth. At least hopeless people recognize that they cannot control the future. At least they recognize their need. Perhaps this is why the author of Ecclesiastes associates wisdom with despair (Ecclesiastes 1:12-18). The wise person, with a realistic view of the world, is filled with grief and sorrow.

> *God is wise, has made known some of His wisdom to us, and in His wisdom God is working all things to good.*

Hopelessness in ourselves, however, should lead to hope in God. We can have a renewed sense of confidence. That confidence, however, is attained through humility and trust in our wise God.

> *Trust in the LORD with all your heart and lean not on your own understanding; in all your ways acknowledge him, and he will make your paths straight.*
> **- Proverbs 3:5-6 (ESV)**

> **Watch Chip Ingram's Teaching and fill in the notes below.**
>
> ▶ **The Wisdom of God**

> *To believe actively that our Heavenly Father constantly spreads around us providential circumstances that work for our present good and our everlasting well-being brings to the soul a veritable benediction. Most of us go through life praying a little, planning a little, jockeying for position, hoping but never being quite certain of anything, and always secretly afraid that we will miss the way. This is a tragic waste of truth and never gives rest to the heart.*
> - A.W. Tozer, The Knowledge of the Holy

What a difference it would make in life's most difficult times if we could but believe that God is "all wise!"

Defining the Wisdom of God

Definition: "That attribute of God whereby He produces the best possible results by the best possible means" – Berkhof, Systematic Theology

- "the quality of being wise; power of judging rightly and following the soundest course of action based on knowledge, experience, and understanding." Root words - "to see, to know" – Websters

> *But the wisdom from above is first pure, then peaceable, gentle, reasonable, full of mercy and good fruits, unwavering, without hypocrisy.*
> - James 3:17 (NASB)

> *Oh, the depth of the riches of the wisdom and knowledge of God! How unsearchable His judgments, and His paths beyond tracing out!*
> - Romans 11:33

"Wisdom, among other things, is the ability to devise perfect ends and to achieve those ends by the most perfect means. It sees the end from the beginning, so there can be no need to guess or conjecture. All God's acts are done in perfect wisdom, first for His own glory, and then for the highest good of the greatest number for the longest time... Not only could His acts not be better done, a better way to do them could not be imagined."
- A.W. Tozer, The Knowledge of the Holy

How Has God Revealed His Wisdom to Us?

- Through _____ – *Psalm 104:24*
- Through _____ – *Psalm 33:10-11*
- Through _____

> *We do, however, speak a message of wisdom among the mature, but not the wisdom of this age or of the rulers of this age, who are coming to nothing. No, we declare God's wisdom, a mystery that has been hidden and that God destined for our glory before time began. None of the rulers of this age understood it, for if they had, they would not have crucified the Lord of glory. However, as it is written: "What no eye has seen, what no ear has heard, and what no human mind has conceived"—the things God has prepared for those who love him—these are the things God has revealed to us by his Spirit. The Spirit searches all things, even the deep things of God.*
> **- 1 Corinthians 2:6-10**

- Through His _____

> *It is because of him that you are in Christ Jesus, who has become for us wisdom from God—that is, our righteousness, holiness and redemption.*
> **- 1 Corinthians 1:30**

The Wisdom of God

The wisdom of God tells us that God will bring about the best possible results, by the best possible means, for the most possible people, for the longest possible time. **- Dr. Charles Ryrie**

CHAPTER FIVE

How Must We Respond to the Wisdom of God?

We must learn to _____ wisely! *Ephesians 5:15-17*

HOW?

1. 1. It begins with _____ for God's ways. *Proverbs 1:7; Job 28:28*

2. It grows with _____ His Word. *Psalm 119:97-100; 2 Timothy 3:16-17*

3. It _____ asking for it specifically. *James 1:5; Colossians 1:9*

We must learn to _____ completely; that all that comes our way is from the hand of a good and loving God who, knowing all things actual and possible, is exerting His unlimited power to execute the best possible outcomes by the best possible means to fulfill the highest possible purposes.

The Wisdom of God

The following questions will help you reflect on what you watched on the video. If you are in a group spend some time sharing with others.

1. James 3:17 (NASB) says, *"But the wisdom from above is first pure, then peaceable, gentle, reasonable, full of mercy and good fruits, unwavering, without hypocrisy."* In this passage James gives us the characteristics of God's wisdom. What do you need to do right now to become wise?

2. Chip compared life and God's wisdom to a tapestry. On one side it is messy and filled with loose threads and knots. But on the other side is a beautiful design. What is something in your life that felt messy and tangled but now you are able to see how it was part of God's beautiful design?

3. Read 1 Corinthians 2:6-10. What word or phrase most stands out to you? Why?

4. 1 Corinthians 1:30 says, *"It is because of him that you are in Christ Jesus, who has become for us wisdom from God—that is, our righteousness, holiness and redemption."* What does righteousness, holiness and redemption, have to do with wisdom?

5. Ephesians 5:15-17 (NIV) says, *"Be very careful, then, how you live—not as unwise but as wise, making the most of every opportunity, because the days are evil. Therefore do not be foolish, but understand what the Lord's will is."* In order for you to live "wisely," what is one area where you need to be careful how you live?

6. Read Psalm 119:97-100. God's wisdom is most clearly revealed in Scripture. What step could you take to more deeply take in the wisdom of God in Scripture?

In Colossians 1:9 (NIV) Paul says, *"We continually ask God to fill you with the knowledge of his will through all the wisdom and understanding that the Spirit gives."* Is there anything going on in your life right now where you need the wisdom of God? Share that with the group and then spend some time praying for these needs.

Discovering Wisdom

This next section is for you to complete on your own. Take what you have learned and turn it into action.

The Folly of Humankind

When we look at our world we see much that reflects God's wisdom as Creator. However, this world has one blatant example of foolishness. It's the one creature in our physical world to which we rightly apply the term **"folly."*** We don't call animals foolish. We reserve that word for humans.

The folly of human beings has been a theme of some of the great works of literature. The following are just a few notable examples: Cervantes' Don Quixote, Chaucer's Canterbury Tales, and Shakespeare's King Lear. Folly is a wonderful source of comedy. We often see folly portrayed in contemporary TV and movie characters like Inspector Clouseau (played by both Peter Sellers and Steve Martin) in the Pink Panther movies, Lucille Ball's Lucy, and Rowan Atikinson's character Mr. Bean.

How do you tend to respond to foolish characters in literature, film, or TV?

○ I feel sorry for them

○ I can see myself doing the same thing and not realizing my folly

○ I find them lovable

○ I'm glad not to be them

○ I don't find them funny at all

Folly, noun. — the absence of good judgment; without discretion; madness

Unfortunately, the folly of humankind is not limited to characters in literature or on screen. We exhibit plenty of folly in real life. It's also not limited to instances when it is funny and harmless. Human folly can be painful and costly. We're going to look at a biblical character who exhibits a great deal of foolishness, especially in light of the wisdom of God he repeatedly received. This character is Abraham—someone not often associated with folly.

God's Wisdom and Abraham's Folly

In His first recorded communication with Abram (later renamed Abraham), God included a promise to make Abram into a great nation:

> *The LORD had said to Abram, "Leave your country, your people and your father's household and go to the land I will show you. I will make you into a great nation and I will bless you."*
> **- Genesis 12:1-2**

> *After Abram enters the land, God shows up and provides further information: "To your offspring I will give this land" (Genesis 12:7,). In case it was unclear the Lord specifies that Abram's heir will be an "offspring"— or literally his seed. God repeats the message. He tells Abram that "a son coming from your own body will be your heir."*
> **- Genesis 15:4**

With that settled, attention turns to the mother of the promised child. Let's see how the story unfolds next in Genesis 16:

> *Now Sarai, Abram's wife, had borne him no children. But she had an Egyptian maidservant named Hagar; so she said to Abram, "The LORD has kept me from having children. Go, sleep with my maidservant; perhaps I can build a family through her." Abram agreed to what Sarai said.*
> **- Genesis 16:1-2**

Which of the following statements are accurate regarding the broader context of Genesis 16:1-2? *(Circle those you think are true.)*

- a. God instructed Abram to have a child by Hagar
- b. Sarai and Abram followed local custom and law
- c. Sarai and Abram sought God's will in prayer
- d. God condemned the son born to Hagar

(See the answer on the bottom of this page.)

Abram's decision to follow the advice of Sarai proves very unwise. He took matters into his own hands, rather than patiently waiting on God's lead. Not only is this son not God's plan for an heir for Abram, it creates havoc in his home life as Sarai becomes jealous of Hagar.

God's next communication with Abram is even more blunt (Genesis 17:15-16). The son, He states, will come from Sarai (who is later renamed Sarah). How does Abraham respond to this?

> *Abraham fell facedown; he laughed and said to himself, "Will a son be born to a man a hundred years old? Will Sarah bear a child at the age of ninety?"*
> **- Genesis 17:17**

Have you ever had a reaction of both reverence and laughter when faced with what appeared to be God's plan for your life? —An experience that made you feel like saying, "With all due respect God, You can't be serious."

Describe that experience:

_____

_____

_____

_____

(Answer: b & c. Regarding (d), God actually made provision for Hagar and her son to survive with promise of his descendants becoming a great nation, see Genesis. 21:8-21.)

How did you respond and what did you learn about God and His wisdom in hindsight?

_____

_____

_____

To Abraham's questions in Genesis 17:17, God's answer seems to be: "Yes Abraham, in fact that is my plan."

Abraham laughed at God's wise plan, but Sarah has her moment later on. After God returns to tell Abraham that he will have a son by Sarah within a year's time, Sarah overhears and also laughs (Genesis 18:10-12). Notice how God responds:

> *Then the LORD said to Abraham, "Why did Sarah laugh and say, 'Will I really have a child, now that I am old?' Is anything too hard for the LORD? I will return to you at the appointed time next year and Sarah will have a son."*
> **- Genesis 18:13-14**

In Genesis 21:3, the son comes and Abraham names him Isaac, meaning "he laughs." This is often taken to refer to both the laughter of Abraham and Sarah from Genesis 17 and 18 and the joyous laughter that his birth brings to his parents. Perhaps there is a bit of irony in the name Isaac as well. Perhaps Abraham is laughing at himself and his impatient attempts to supersede God's wisdom. Perhaps the name reflects God getting the last laugh. In any case, Abraham's flawed wisdom to secure a son turns out to be folly. God's wisdom triumphs.

Abraham's Son, Ishmael

The following are some of the consequences that Abraham and his descendants would experience as a result of his unwise decision to have a son by Sarah's maidservant:

- Ishmael's descendants "lived in hostility" with Abraham's son Isaac and his descendants (Genesis. 25:18)
- Esau took a daughter of Ishmael to try to please his parents after having taken Canaanite women as wives.
- A group Ishmaelites bought Joseph as a slave and took him to Egypt. (Genesis. 37:25-28)

In the bigger picture of human history, how would you describe the difference that it has made that God's wisdom and not Abraham's won the day?

_____

_____

_____

_____

God's Wisdom in the Cross

We now turn to an even greater example of God's wisdom. We'll see that trusting God's wisdom can be even more costly than enduring a long awaited son or serving seven months in prison. It can involve severe suffering and the ultimate sacrifice—even suffering that appears to be foolishness.

Take a look at this passage and pay attention to God's wisdom in saving the lost through Christ's work on the cross in contrast to human wisdom. Notice the association of Christ with wisdom. In the passage underline all the instances of foolish or foolishness and wise or wisdom.

> *For the message of the cross is foolishness to those who are perishing, but to us who are being saved it is the power of God. For it is written: "I will destroy the wisdom of the wise; the intelligence of the intelligent I will frustrate." Where is the wise man? Where is the scholar? Where is the philosopher of this age? Has not God made foolish the wisdom of the world? For since in the wisdom of God the world through its wisdom did not know him, God was pleased through the foolishness of what was preached to save those who believe...*
>
> *For the foolishness of God is wiser than man's wisdom, and the weakness of God is stronger than man's strength. Brothers, think of what you were when you were called. Not many of you were wise by human standards; not many were influential; not many were of noble birth.*
>
> *But God chose the foolish things of the world to shame the wise; God chose the weak things of the world to shame the strong. He chose the lowly things of this world and the despised things—and the things that*

are not—to nullify the things that are, so that no one may boast before him. It is because of him that you are in Christ Jesus, who has become for us wisdom from God—that is, our righteousness, holiness and redemption.
- 1 Corinthians 1:18-21, 25-30

List three things you can learn about God's wisdom from this passage:

1. _____

2. _____

3. _____

Living Wisely

Reverence for God

In light of all that we've learned about God's wisdom—a wisdom that is informed by His goodness and His sovereign ability to fulfill His purposes—we can trust God and not lean upon our own limited understanding and flawed judgment.

> *The fear of the LORD is the beginning of wisdom, and knowledge of the Holy One is understanding.*
> **- Proverbs 9:10**

Take the first part of that verse, "The fear of the LORD is the beginning of wisdom." How do you think a fearful reverence of God begins a path of wisdom in our lives?

_____

_____

_____

Receiving God's Wisdom

> *Oh, how I love your law! I meditate on it all day long. Your commands make me wiser than my enemies, for they are ever with me.*
>
> *I have more insight than all my teachers, for I meditate on your statutes. I have more understanding than the elders, for I obey your precepts.*
> **- Psalm 119: 97-100**

As we learned above, God's wisdom is most powerfully revealed to those in desperate need of salvation by means of the work of Christ on the cross. When we fear God, repent of our sins, and place our faith in Christ, we enter into a new way of wisdom. Our lives are now living sacrifices, as we discussed in the previous chapter. We can walk in good works that He has prepared for us. Thus, we can receive God's wisdom now for a life of growing in holiness. That starts with going to the source of God's wisdom—the Bible.

> *All Scripture is God-breathed and is useful for teaching, rebuking, correcting and training in righteousness, so that the man of God may be thoroughly equipped for every good work.*
> **- 2 Timothy 3:16-17**

Let's look at one example of some of the wisdom God has for his redeemed ones.

> *Who is wise and understanding among you? Let him show it by his good life, by deeds done in the humility that comes from wisdom. But if you harbor bitter envy and selfish ambition in your hearts, do not boast about it or deny the truth. Such "wisdom" does not come down from heaven but is earthly, unspiritual, of the devil. For where you have envy and selfish ambition, there you find disorder and every evil practice. But the wisdom that comes from heaven is first of all pure; then peace-loving, considerate, submissive, full of mercy and good fruit, impartial and sincere.*
> **- James 3:13-17**

Describe in your own words the contrast between earthly wisdom and the wisdom "that comes down from heaven."

_____

_____

In light of the description of wisdom in James 3, what are some practical steps you can take this week to live according to godly wisdom rather than earthly wisdom?

_____

_____

Ask for Wisdom

Sometimes our need for wisdom goes beyond the kinds of general instructions we receive from Scripture like those found in James 3. For example, sometimes we face choices between several seemingly good and right options. Or we face situations that are very complicated and not clear-cut.

The following passage is an amazing promise for those who ask God for wisdom:

> *If any of you lacks wisdom, he should ask God, who gives generously to all without finding fault, and it will be given to him. But when he asks, he must believe and not doubt, because he who doubts is like a wave of the sea, blown and tossed by the wind. That man should not think he will receive anything from the Lord; he is a double-minded man, unstable in all he does.*
> **-James 1:5-8**

What normally causes you not to ask God for wisdom?

- ◯ I've got things under control (hubris)
- ◯ It doesn't seem like it will make any difference (hopelessness)
- ◯ I forget to ask
- ◯ I'm afraid He might tell me to do something I won't want to do
- ◯ I doubt my ability to hear God
- ◯ I don't feel I've earned the right to ask Him

What helps increase your faith in God when you ask Him for wisdom?

- ◯ To remember past times when I received wisdom from God
- ◯ To recall examples in Scripture when He gave wisdom to those who asked
- ◯ When I remind myself that He *knows* what is good for me
- ◯ When I remind myself that He *wants* what is good for me
- ◯ When I remind myself that He is in complete control of all things

What are the things you need wisdom for right now? List below those things for which you will commit to asking God for wisdom this week.

_____

_____

_____

We don't have to live with a sense of hopelessness. We can also relinquish our prideful hubris—a misguided confidence in our wisdom alone. There is a way of wisdom. In humility and dependence we have access to the wisdom of God. His wisdom has no limitations. His wisdom provides clear guidance and a confidence that comes from faith. It achieves the best possible results by the best possible means.

Putting Your Response to God in Prayer

Your last step for this week. Taking your list from above, follow James 3 and ask for God's wisdom for your situations. Write out your prayer here and decide in advance to follow whatever direction God provides to you.

CHAPTER **FIVE**

CHAPTER **SIX**
Justice of God

*Clouds and thick darkness surround Him;
righteousness and justice are the foundation of his throne.*

Psalm 97:2

Did They Deserve What They Received?

A beautiful young woman approached the edge of a cliff overlooking a lake. As she playfully leapt into the water below, her dreams came crashing to an end. Joni Eareckson would never stand nor walk again. Since then, she has lived the rest of her days paralyzed from the neck down.

It was the summer before her first year in college. She was a gifted individual with many interests. And she knew God. In her hospital bed she said to a friend, "I just don't get it! I trusted God before my accident. I wasn't a bad person." [1]

We've studied in a previous chapter that God is sovereign over all things. He was in control of Joni's situation. He could have stopped this from happening.

What did Joni do to deserve this?

On November 30, 2001, the largest bankruptcy in U.S. history was filed. The Enron Corporation scandal is one of the most famous business fraud cases of all time. Many of the leadership reaped what they sowed. Their actions resulted in indictments, convictions, and prison.

There was, however, one notable exception to this trail of devastation. Approximately six months before the bankruptcy, a top Enron executive resigned. No one quite knows why. Lou Pai just up and left. Pai was known for being ruthless in business. His adulterous relationship with a club dancer led to his divorce. The divorce proceedings created a need for him to cash out his equity holdings with Enron. He cashed out over $280 million when Enron's stock was approximately $53 per share. Six months later the stock was worthless. [2]

Following his resignation, Pai went on to make profitable real estate investments and got involved in horse breeding. He has never been charged with any crimes in the Enron scandal, though he did plead the Fifth Amendment to avoid having to give testimony. Though he paid one of the largest settlements in history to the Security and Exchange Commission (out of court for $31.5 million), Pai came out of the scandal profiting on a massive scale.

God was just as sovereign over Lou Pai's situation as he was over Joni Eareckson's.

What did Lou Pai do to deserve this?

---

[1] "Joni's Story – Page 1", Accessed Dec 1, 2016. http://joniearecksontadastory.com/jonis-story-page-1/

[2] http://www.npr.org/templates/story/story.php?storyId=5411422
http://www.corpwatch.org/article.php?id=13194

Fair and Equitable Treatment

Fair and equitable treatment is an ideal that is often praised—and for good reason. Getting the same grade for the same quality of work in school or getting equal pay for performance of the same level of professionalism on the job feels good and right and just. Teachers and supervisors who are fair and equitable are trusted and respected. It provides a sense of stability and security to the classroom or the workplace. You know what to expect and appreciate the fair treatment you receive.

We all know what it feels like to receive unfair treatment. Maybe your high school coaches or teachers played favorites. Maybe you've been subject to discrimination or prejudice. Your work colleague gets praise for mediocre work, while you receive no response for high quality work. This lack of fair and equitable treatment by authority figures is unsettling. You don't know what to expect. It's frustrating and you feel helpless to make what's wrong right because an unjust person has authority.

We see this concept of fairness—what is right and what is wrong—in every aspect of our daily lives. It's not only something that comes from authority figures. Friends as well as parents, co-workers as well as employers judge us on where we live up to and where we fall short of their standards. We might be judged for anything from how we dress to how we manage our finances. People universally judge each other. Whenever we are amongst other people, we can be sure that judgments are being made and people are being treated in certain ways according to those judgments, whether justly or unjustly. But, one Judge stands above all...

God is the ultimate Judge.

How much do you struggle with those who "get away with it"?

1   2   3   4   5   6   7   8   9   10

It's just part of life   *Punishment now!*

Write down a circumstance from your own life where you or someone you know got a raw deal.

_____

_____

Getting What We Deserve

The topic of justice involves both rewards and punishments. At a very basic level, justice can be understood as people getting what they deserve. Praiseworthy behavior should result in rewards. Blameworthy behavior, in punishment. What is praiseworthy and blameworthy depends on the person that makes that judgment. Who gets to decide what is right and wrong?

God dispenses His justice in light of His own righteous standards. Let's see what we can learn about those standards and His justice as we turn to the video.

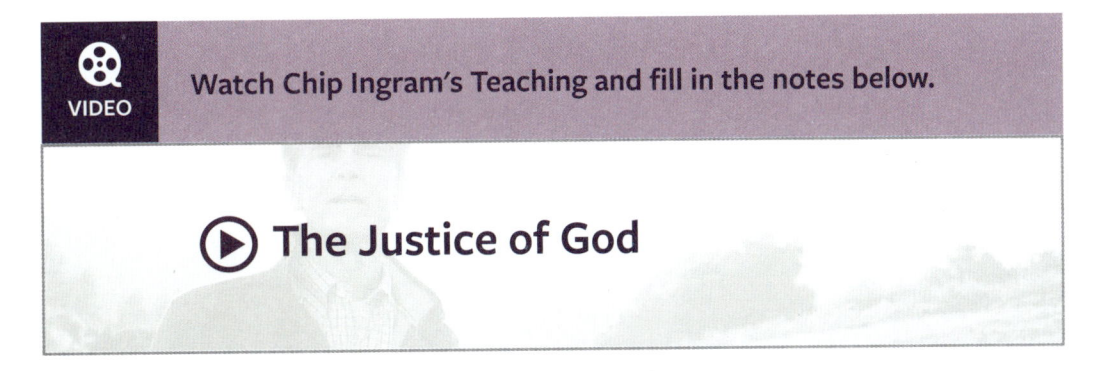

VIDEO — Watch Chip Ingram's Teaching and fill in the notes below.

▶ **The Justice of God**

Introduction: Two Questions that Disturb Believers and Unbelievers Alike

1. Why do bad things happen to good people? 2. Why do good things happen to bad people?

The Real Issue is… "Life's not fair!" The Deeper Issue… Is God _____?

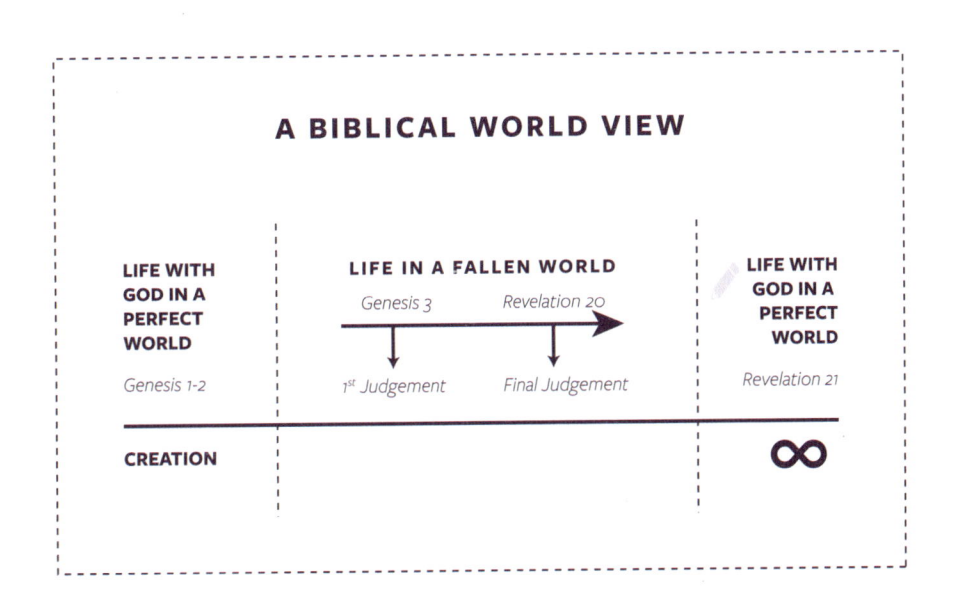

A BIBLICAL WORLD VIEW

LIFE WITH GOD IN A PERFECT WORLD	LIFE IN A FALLEN WORLD	LIFE WITH GOD IN A PERFECT WORLD
Genesis 1-2	Genesis 3 → Revelation 20	Revelation 21
CREATION	1st Judgement … Final Judgement	∞

Defining The Justice of God

- Revealed through Abraham

> *"Far be it from you to do such a thing—to kill the righteous with the wicked, treating the righteous and the wicked alike. Far be it from you! Will not the Judge of all the earth do right?"*
> **- Genesis 18:25**

- Revealed through the Psalmist

> *"Clouds and thick darkness surround Him; righteousness and justice are the foundation of His throne."*
> **- Psalm 97:2**

> *"Justice embodies the idea of moral equity... Judgment is the application of equity to moral situations and may be favorable or unfavorable according to whether the one under examination has been equitable or inequitable in heart and conduct."*
> **- A.W. Tozer, Knowledge of the Holy**

> *"...God's work as Judge is part of His character... It shows us also that the heart of the justice which expresses God's nature is retribution, the rendering to men, what they have deserved; for this is the essence of the judge's task. To reward good with good, and evil with evil, is natural to God. So, when the New Testament speaks of the final judgment, it always represents it in terms of retribution. God will judge all men, it says, 'according to their works'- (Matthew 16:27; Revelation 20:12f)."*
> **- J. I. Packer, Knowing God**

How Does God Reveal His Justice to Us?

- Through the Natural Order - *Romans 1:18-20*

- Through the _____ _____ - *Romans 2:15-16*

  > "These, then are the two points I wanted to make. First, that human beings, all over the earth, have this curious idea that they ought to behave in a certain way, and cannot really get rid of it. Secondly, that they do not in fact behave in that way. They know the Law of Nature; they break it. These two facts are the foundation of all clear thinking about ourselves and the universe we live in."
  > **-C.S. Lewis, Mere Christianity**

- Through His Role as _____ - *Hebrews 12:23; 2 Timothy 4:8; John 5:22*

- Through the _____ - *Romans 3:25-26*

  > "For Christ also died for sins, once for all, the just for the unjust, so that He might bring us to God, having been put to death in the flesh, but made alive in the spirit;"
  > **- 1 Peter 3:18 (NASB)**

- Through the Promise of Eternal _____.
  - For Believers - *1 Corinthians 3:10-15*
  - For Unbelievers - *Hebrews 9:27*

How Are We to Respond to God's Justice?

- _____ to embrace Jesus today as your Savior rather than meet Him as your righteous judge later. *John 5:22-24; 1 Peter 3:18*

- _____ to take revenge when treated unjustly knowing God and God alone is judge. *Romans 12:17-21*

- _____ deeply your time, talent, and treasure in view of the "judgment seat of Christ" and the injustices in our world. *2 Corinthians 5:10; 1 Corinthians 3:10-15*

The Justice of God

The following questions will help you reflect on what you watched on the video. If you are in a group spend some time sharing with others.

1. Read 1 Corinthians 3:10-15. As you consider the passage and the teaching in this session, what most stands out to you? Why?

2. Psalm 97:2 says, *"Righteousness and justice are the foundation of His throne."* What do you think this statement means?

3. When speaking about the Cross, Chip said, *"What the holiness/justice of God demanded, the love of God provided."* How would you explain that statement?

4. Read Revelation 20:11-15. This Great White Throne judgment is the final retribution for all who have rejected Christ. What most stands out to you from this passage? How should the reality of this judgment impact how we live?

5. Read Romans 12:14-21. Which phrase or verse do you most need to apply in your own life?

6. As Christ followers, we should reflect the character of God. Since God is just we should care about justice. What injustice most bothers you and makes you angry?

Spend some time praying about some of the injustices that came up during your discussion time. Intercede on behalf of those who are experiencing oppression and injustice.

CHAPTER SIX

The Justice of God in a Broken World

NEXT STEPS

This next section is for you to complete on your own. Take what you have learned and turn it into action.

Cutting the line

It's enough to make your blood boil... You've been waiting what seems like an eternity in a long line of traffic. And then, cars start driving up the shoulder and cutting in at the front of the line. With every fiber of your being, you want to lash out. You know that cars cutting in line are not going to lead to the collapse of civilization. It's not going to ruin your life. But, you also know that it's just wrong.

If you take some time to observe and listen to the way people talk in every day life, it doesn't take you long to realize that people make judgments all the time. They make judgments about the way people work. They make judgments about the way people communicate. About the way people spend money. Some of these judgments are superficial, but some are not. Some of the judgments are made with deep conviction. Some are so deep that the judgment appeals to a universal sense of justice. That's just wrong!

For example, it's just wrong for a parent to abandon a child. It's inexcusable no matter what the context

Make a list of several practices that people judge to be unjust. They could be practices within your own society or practices that are observed around the world.

_____

_____

_____

_____

Some practices are so extremely unjust that they are easy to identify and condemn. Activist movements have mobilized many thousands of impassioned supporters to fight blatant injustices such as slavery, sex trafficking, domestic abuse, and abortion. These injustices remind us that a universal standard of right and wrong exists, and human beings fail to live up to it.

THE REAL GOD WORKBOOK | *Living On The Edge*

89

Starting Your Own Company

Imagine that you have started your own company. Maybe the company produces a new type of airbag for vehicles or a new drug to cure Parkinson's disease. The idea of the company was birthed in your mind; you built it from the ground up. In the process, you discovered that there were some crucial practices that had to be executed consistently in order to ensure the safety of your employees, as well as to meet the needs of your customers. If your employees do those things, your customers will benefit. If they don't, your employees and customers will be put at risk.

So, you train your employees rigorously, stressing the importance of those practices. You are confident that they know the importance of those practices and have everything they need to faithfully execute those practices. Now imagine that you show up to work one day and observe blatant disregard for those practices among the employees.

How would you feel? What thoughts would go through your mind?
(Check all that you apply.)

Emotions:	Thoughts:
○ Anger	○ "People are going to get hurt"
○ Anxiety	○ "How could they do this to me?"
○ Fear	○ "It'll be ok"
○ Joy	○ "I've got to warn our customers"
○ Satisfaction	○ "Things like this happen"
○ Disappointment	○ "Maybe they're just exploring a better way to do it"
○ Excitement	○ "They know better than this"
○ Frustration	○ "I've got to put a stop to this right now"
○ Other	○ "Someone is about to get fired!"
	○ Other: _____

You worked hard to figure out the best way to produce something that made customer's lives safer or healthier. You made sure that neither employees nor customers would be at risk—only to find that your instructions were ignored and the well-being of people was threatened.

Imagine how God must feel. He has created something far more significant and far more intricate. He has created an amazing and complex world. He has entrusted human beings with an enormous responsibility to manage it, as well as their own lives. Yet, we fail in so many ways. And the consequences of our failures are enormous. Let's look at some ways that God has made clear what practices lead to healthy individuals and communities. Our Maker has outlined what is required of us—the practices that lead to personal health, healthy relationships, and a healthy world. From these, let's see what we can discern about the justice of God.

The Ten Commandments

The setting is Mt. Sinai. A great host of Hebrews are meeting their Creator. The great I AM is in their midst. He's working to shape them into a holy people. After giving them four commands for how they are to honor and relate to Him, God gives them six commands that spell out the foundational principles for how they are to live and relate to each other.

> "Honor your father and your mother, so that you may live long in the land the LORD your God is giving you.
> You shall not murder.
> You shall not commit adultery.
> You shall not steal.
> You shall not give false testimony against your neighbor.
> You shall not covet your neighbor's house. You shall not covet your neighbor's wife, or his manservant or maidservant, his ox or donkey, or anything that belongs to your neighbor."
> - Exodus 20: 12-17

How strict or difficult do these six commands seem to you? (*Rating with 5 being most strict or difficult.*)

1 — 2 — 3 — 4 — 5

How likely would you be to obey all of them...
(Rating with 5 being most likely to obey.)

- **In the next 24 hours:**

  1 —— 2 —— 3 —— 4 —— 5

- **In the next month:**

  1 —— 2 —— 3 —— 4 —— 5

- **In the next year:**

  1 —— 2 —— 3 —— 4 —— 5

It doesn't take long to understand that these moral principles present us with an extremely challenging vision to live up to. Those Hebrews and their descendants would learn just how difficult God's instructions were, as they consistently failed to obey. And in case this vision for our moral lives wasn't difficult enough, Jesus came onto the scene and gave us the Father's authorized interpretation of those commands.

Here are just a few examples of Jesus' interpretation:

> *You have heard that it was said to the people long ago, 'Do not murder, and anyone who murders will be subject to judgment.' But I tell you that anyone who is angry with his brother will be subject to judgment.*
> **- Matthew 5:21-22**

> *You have heard that it was said, 'Do not commit adultery.' But I tell you that anyone who looks at a woman lustfully has already committed adultery with her in his heart.*
> **- Matthew 5:27-28**

How do these interpretations of two of the Ten Commandments inform our understanding of how God judges our lives?

_____

_____

_____

You probably noticed that Jesus leaves no doubt that God judges not only behavior but also the motive and intent of our actions. God's justice is not satisfied with shallow religiosity (Matthew 15:18-20). Instead, the justice of God takes into consideration the dynamics of the human heart. No other judge is like Him. He sees and He knows the innermost aspects of our lives (Psalm 139:1-4).

We see an example of penetrating justice of God in Jesus' judgments of the Pharisees. They diligently ordered their lives to prove that they were righteous—that they were good people on the outside. But, Jesus gives them a blunt warning:

> *The Pharisees, who loved money, heard all this and were sneering at Jesus. He said to them, "You are the ones who justify yourselves in the eyes of men, but God knows your hearts."*
> - Luke 16:14-15

God doesn't just know the hearts of the Pharisees, but ours, as well. God knows every individual, and everyone will be evaluated according to His just standards (Romans 14:10, 12).

The justice of God at the Cross

It doesn't take much to realize that our lives have no hope of measuring up to God's standard. The core problem is that we have poisoned hearts. Our hearts are infected with sin, and the prognosis is not good. Thus, the prospect of standing before the throne of God presents us with what appears like a hopeless situation. We can no more remove the guilt of our past sin than we can will our way to a sinless life in the present. He is the judge over all things including each of us. He cannot and will not overlook our sin. We deserve to be punished for our sin and the just punishment is eternal separation from God. God will not abide sin in His presence.

As we learned in the gospel of John already, we all stand condemned before God (John 3:18, 36). We also see our hopeless condition expressed in Ephesians 2:3.

All of us also lived among them at one time, gratifying the cravings of our sinful nature and following its desires and thoughts. Like the rest, we were by nature objects of wrath.

You might wonder why God's swift judgment has not yet been unleashed. As we observe the ravaging effects of sin constantly reeking havoc in our homes and neighborhoods, as well around the world, a deep frustration can set in. Along with the Psalmist, you might want to express to God in frustration:

> *Rise up, O Judge of the earth; pay back to the proud what they deserve. How long will the wicked, O LORD, how long will the wicked be jubilant?*
> **- Psalm 94:2-3**

However, God has already poured out His wrath in judgment upon the wicked. His justice has been satisfied, at least in part. At one defining moment in history, God poured out divine punishment on sin and His justice was satisfied.

> *[Jesus] sacrificed for their sins once for all when He offered Himself.*
> **- Hebrews 7:27**

Consider Jesus' sacrifice with fresh eyes: The perfect Son of God received upon Himself the wrath of God that you and I deserved. The cross is a profound demonstration of the justice of God (Romans 3:22-26). God's justice demanded a costly price, and the price was paid.

Justice was satisfied as Christ received the punishment for our sin and, through our identification with Him, we receive His righteousness. The Father no longer sees our sins, but rather sees the righteousness of Christ when He sees us. John assures us that Jesus' payment was enough to cover not only our sins, but also the sins of all humankind:

> *He is the atoning sacrifice for our sins, and not only for ours but also for the sins of the whole world.*
> **- 1 John 2:2**

The Discipline of the Father

Having seen how God's justice was at work redeeming us through Christ, we can now see how God's justice works to grow us in holiness. Driven by His vision for us to be holy, God disciplines us. The imagery Scripture uses is that of a father disciplining a son.

> *My son, do not make light of the Lord's discipline, and do not lose heart when he rebukes you, because the Lord disciplines those he loves, and he punishes everyone he accepts as a son...*
>
> *Our fathers disciplined us for a little while as they thought best; but God disciplines us for our good, that we may share in his holiness. No discipline seems pleasant at the time, but painful. Later on, however, it produces a harvest of righteousness and peace for those who have been trained by it.*
> **- Hebrews 12:5-6, 10-11**

The Judgments of a Parent

Every parent has experienced something like this:

The child insists that he did not knock over the vase, but there it lies shattered on the floor.

You soon discover that there's no one else around, no other possible explanation. It was him. You could let it go, thinking, "It's no big deal." But, you feel compelled to think it through—to make a judgment about his actions.

How serious would you rate the child's wrongdoing? *(Rank based on 5 being the most serious)*

Breaking the vase: 1 — 2 — 3 — 4 — 5

Lying about the vase: 1 — 2 — 3 — 4 — 5

I suspect you have judged that the loss of the vase is insignificant in comparison to the loss of your child's honesty. You are frustrated that he didn't tell you the truth, but you get even more disturbed when you play out in your mind a teenaged boy telling you he missed his curfew because he had to help someone on the side of the road when he was driving home. You imagine that you'll have no degree of trust in his story. You envision further into the future when he explains to his boss how it was a colleague who undermined the project.

As these thoughts rush through your mind, you are convinced that discipline is needed. You hate the thought of how sad or angry he will be with his punishments. Yet, you know that discipline for him now will lead to blessing in his future.

Returning to the passage in Hebrew 12, notice that the discipline of God flows out of His plans for our good. Remember back in the Goodness of God chapter, we observed that God works for our good in all things. This is true even in His active discipline. Notice what we gain: "a harvest of righteousness and peace." It's no small thing to reap those when we remember that we started out as condemned sinners.

Final Judgment

God has judged our sin at the cross, and by His just judgments, He disciplines us. So, what now? Does that mean we've accounted for all the aspects of God's justice? Unfortunately, no. There is also a final judgment coming for those who do not receive Christ's sacrificial act for themselves. Since they have not been justified in God's eyes through Christ, their sin remains and, therefore, they remain under condemnation. A sad and terrible judgment awaits them. We can recall again:

> *Whoever believes in the Son has eternal life, but whoever rejects the Son will not see life, for God's wrath remains on him.*
> **- John 3:36**

That might seem a bit harsh. But, consider that Scripture tells us God does not take any pleasure in the condemnation of unbelievers.

> *Do I take any pleasure in the death of the wicked? declares the Sovereign LORD. Rather, am I not pleased when they turn from their ways and live?... "Therefore, O house of Israel, I will judge you, each one according to his ways, declares the Sovereign LORD. Repent! Turn away from all your offenses; then sin will not be your downfall. Rid yourselves of all the offenses you have committed, and get a new heart and a new spirit. Why will you die, O house of Israel? For I take no pleasure in the death of anyone, declares the Sovereign LORD. Repent and live!*
> **- Ezekiel 18:23, 30-32**

This passage gives us an important reminder that God wants nothing more than for the lost to repent and be saved. He has given us choices. We make choices to sin and fall under condemnation in light of His just judgments. But we also have the choice of faith. By faith in the Son, we can be saved from this condemnation. Unfortunately, not all make the choice of faith as they reject the Son. His justice is right and equitable, but it is terrible and sorrowful when the lost refuse His offer of justification.

No matter how much some people seem to get away with their sin in this world. No matter how much they may treat others unjustly or indulge in sinful practices without seeming to pay the price, God's judgment is coming. We will all face the throne of God to be judged.

Choose to Embrace Jesus

The first crucial action step to take is to repent and receive forgiveness for your sin if you have never done so. Take to heart these two verses, and come to God in repentance:

> *I tell you the truth, whoever hears my word and believes Him who sent me has eternal life and will not be condemned; he has crossed over from death to life.*
> **- John 5:24**

> *For Christ died for sins once for all, the righteous for the unrighteous, to bring you to God.*
> **- 1 Peter 3:18**

If you have already repented and been saved from condemnation through Christ:

Describe one concrete thing you will do this week to remind yourself that you have been saved from condemnation through faith in Christ.

Refuse to Take Revenge Against the Unjust

One of the important implications of recognizing God as the ultimate judge of human beings is recognizing that we are not. Romans 12:19 assures us that we can trust God to judge and urges believers to relinquish any personal plans of punishing injustice ourselves:

> *Do not take revenge, my friends, but leave room for God's wrath, for it is written: "It is mine to avenge; I will repay," says the Lord.*
> **- Romans 12:19**

That means there is no room for holding grudges, or worse. Lashing out in vengeance is not part of God's calling for our lives. God will take care of injustices with just judgments and in His timing.

List any injustices that you or people you love have experienced that cause you to hold a grudge or make you desire vengeance:

In light of Romans 12:19, what steps will you take this week to relinquish those to the justice of God?

Investing Your Life in Light of God's Judgment

Ponder how you are investing your time, talent and treasure in life. Though all believers will be saved from condemnation, Chip pointed out in the video that we face God's judgment for how we lived our lives in faith. Paul urges that we pay attention to how we live in light of that judgment:

> *But each one should be careful how he builds... his work will be shown for what it is, because the Day will bring it to light. It will be revealed with fire, and the fire will test the quality of each man's work. If what he has built survives, he will receive his reward.*
> **- 1 Corinthians 3:10, 13-14**

What plans will you set into motion this week to change or refine the way you invest your time, talent and treasure so that your works will have eternal consequences and you will be justly rewarded?

The justice of God is terrifying when we think of how far short we fall of His moral standards for our lives. Thanks be to God that the just condemnation of our sins fell upon our Savior, Jesus Christ! It was His love—His desire to redeem His lost children—that motivated this great salvation of believers. We will learn more about that love in the next chapter.

Putting Your Response to God in Prayer

We can be confident that God is just; ultimately every action in history will be judged by God. Are there areas of injustice that have turned to bitterness for you? It's been said that bitterness is like drinking poison and hoping the other person gets sick. Write a prayer to release any past issues of injustice you have experienced to God.

CHAPTER **SEVEN**
Love of God

See what great love the Father has lavished on us, that we should be called children of God! And that is what we are!

1 John 3:1

CHAPTER SEVEN

The Love of a Parent for a Child

Contemporary society often portrays the love of a parent for their children as the deepest and most authentic form of love. We might assume that it's a universal fact that parents love their children. Though tragically, we know it's not always true.

While there are gut wrenching examples of parents who simply do not love their children, much more common is the case of parents whose attempts to love are not received as loving by the child. There is a disconnection between the parent's desire and efforts to love and the child feeling loved. Those disconnects can involve:

- The parent failing to express their love in ways that the child will understand as loving.
- The parent is pursuing the best interest of the child in ways that the child is unable to understand.

How loved did you feel by your parents at the time of your youth? *(Rank based on 5 being most loved)*

1 — 2 — 3 — 4 — 5

How loved do you feel by your parents as you look back now? *(Rank based on 5 being most loved)*

1 — 2 — 3 — 4 — 5

Describe what made you feel loved and what did not make you feel loved.

_____
_____
_____
_____

Parents have to be intentional about assuring their child that their love is unconditional. They don't want the child to feel loved only as long as they do what they want them to do.

As the parent consistently pursues the best interest of the child it will become more and more evident to the child that the parent's actions are motivated by love. The child will be assured of the parent's love even after being punished. Again, the child may not be able to express this, but they will sense the parent's steadfast love and come to rely upon that love—even take it for granted.

On the other hand, if the relationship is consistently built around the child receiving affection and love that is dependent on good behavior, the child can naturally assume that the parent's love is conditional.

The example of parent and child is one of the most common analogies in the Bible of the relationship between God the Father and us. It's no surprise. In the same way that the parents' love for their child is not always perceived as loving, we sometimes don't feel that God is loving us. However, this cannot be attributed to any lack of love on His part to love us. While the parental love might be a good analogy of God's love, it is only a faint one. It can never come close to the inexhaustible love of God. If there's one thing about God we don't need to doubt, its His love.

VIDEO — Watch Chip Ingram's Teaching and fill in the notes below.`

▶ **The Love of God**

FACT #1: It's a universal need = We are all looking for love!

FACT #2: There's a universal solution = God loves all people everywhere and longs to meet the deepest needs of their heart for love!

FACT #3: There's a tragic disconnection = Nevertheless, most people remain starved for love for three primary reasons:

1. They don't know God loves them.
2. They know of God's love, but have not received it.
3. They have received God's love, but don't know how to experience it in daily life.

CHAPTER SEVEN

> *How great is the love the Father has lavished on us that we should be called the children of God! And that is what we are!*
> - 1 John 3:1

Defining the Love of God

Definition: God's love is His holy disposition toward all that He has created that compels Him to express unconditional affection and selective correction to provide the highest and best quality of existence both now and forever for the objects of His love. Characteristics of God's agape love include:

- It is a giving love - *John 3:16*
- It is a sacrificial love - *John 3:16*
- It is an unconditional love - *John 3:16*
- It is a boundless love - *Ephesians 3:14-21*

Love is giving another person what they need the most, when they deserve it the least, at great personal cost.

God's love for you means...

1. His thoughts, intentions, desires, and plans for you are always for your good and never for your harm.

2. He is kind, open, approachable, frank, and eager to be your friend.

3. He emotionally identifies with your pain, joy, hopes, and dreams, and has chosen to allow your happiness to affect His own.

4. He takes pleasure in you just for who you are, totally apart from your performance and/or accomplishments.

5. He is actively and creatively orchestrating people, circumstances, and events to express His affection and selective correction to provide for your highest good.

CHAPTER SEVEN

God Reveals His Love to Us Through…

- _____ – He made you for Himself *Genesis 1:26-27; Colossians 1:16*

- _____ – He shows His kindness to all. *Matthew 5:44-45; Acts 17:24-27*

- _____ – He is proactively pursuing you. *Luke 19:10; John 4:23-24*

- _____ – He chastises us to protect us from self-destructive behavior. *Hebrews 12:6*

- _____ – He supernaturally pours His love into our hearts by the Holy Spirit. *Romans 5:5*

- _____ – God the Son revealed the nature of God's love for us.
    - Jesus' life modeled compassion, grace, and truth. *John 1:14*
    - Jesus' teaching explained God's love. *Luke 15*
    - Jesus' death demonstrated the extent of God's love. *1 John 3:16; Romans 5:8*

But God demonstrates His own love for us in this: while we were still sinners, Christ died for us. Romans 5:8 _____ _____ _____

An object's value is always determined by the price paid for it. To God, you are worth the price of His Son's death in your place.

How Must We Respond to God's Love?

- We must _____ by faith in our hearts. Yet to all who received Him, to those who believe in His name, He gave the right to become children of God—John 1:12
- We must _____ by faith in our minds.

For I am convinced that neither death, nor life, nor angels, nor principalities, nor things present, nor things to come, nor powers, nor height, nor depth, nor any other created thing, will be able to separate us from the love of God, which is in Christ Jesus our Lord. Romans 8:38-39

- We must _____ by faith through our wills.

Dear children, let us not love with words or speech but with actions and in truth. 1 John 3:18

The Love of God

The following questions will help you reflect on what you watched on the video. If you are in a group spend some time sharing with others.

6. When and how do you still believe God loves you when your performance is bad? Share when you have experienced God's love when you really don't deserve it?

7. On a scale of 1-10 how much do you feel and experience and sense that you are loved by God? Explain.

8. Chip talked about a Performance based vs. grace based view of God's love. It is the belief that you need to act in a certain way to get God's love vs. believing that you are unconditionally loved. What has been your personal journey with this?

9. Chip said that God's love for you means...

   - His thoughts, intentions, desires, and plans for you are always for your good and never for your harm.
   - He is kind, open, approachable, frank, and eager to be your friend.
   - He emotionally identifies with your pain, joy, hopes, and dreams, and has chosen to allow your happiness to affect His own.
   - He takes pleasure in you just for who you are, totally apart from your performance and/or accomplishments.
   - He is actively and creatively orchestrating people, circumstances, and events to express His affection and selective correction to provide for your highest good.
   - Which one of these is most difficult for you to believe? Why?

10. Read Hebrews 12:4-11. The writer of Hebrews talks about discipline as a sign of God's love. What most stands out to you from this passage? Why?

11. Read the story of the Prodigal Son from Luke 15:11-32. What do you notice most about God's love in this passage?

12. 1 John 3:18 says Dear children, let us not love with words or speech but with actions and in truth. We are to be conduits of God's love. What is one practical step you are willing to take this week to demonstrate God's love to somebody in your world?

As you close your group time in prayer, spend a few minutes just thanking God for his unconditional, lavish love that He has poured into our lives.

CHAPTER **SEVEN**

NEXT STEPS

The Pervasive Love of God

> *What a man desires is unfailing love.*
> **- Proverbs 19:11**

Be honest. How loved do you feel by God right now?

1 — 2 — 3 — 4 — 5 — 6 — 7 — 8 — 9 — 10
○   ○   ○   ○   ○   ○   ○   ○   ○   ○

Not Feeling It   **My Cup is Overflowing**

Singing of God's Love

Have you ever heard it said that the God of the Old Testament is a God of judgment but the God of the New Testament is a God of love? While many people tend to think that God is somehow less loving in the Old Testament, those who wrote the Psalms would clearly disagree. Let's take a look at just some of the song lyrics written by those psalmists so many centuries ago.

> *Remember, O LORD, your great mercy and love, for they are from of old. Remember not the sins of my youth and my rebellious ways; according to your love remember me, for you are good, O LORD.*
> **- Psalm 25:6-7**

> *Your love, O LORD, reaches to the heavens, your faithfulness to the skies... How priceless is your unfailing love! Both high and low among men find refuge in the shadow of your wings.*
> **- Psalm 36:5,7**

> *When I said, "My foot is slipping," your love, O LORD, supported me. When anxiety was great within me, your consolation brought joy to my soul.*
> **- Psalm 94:18-19**

CHAPTER **SEVEN**

> *The LORD is compassionate and gracious, slow to anger, abounding in love.*
> **- Psalm 103:8**

> *Give thanks to the LORD, for he is good; his love endures forever.*
> **- Psalm 106:1**

Below describe five things you observe about the love of God from these verses in the Psalms:

1. _____
2. _____
3. _____
4. _____
5. _____

How does it make you feel when you read about God's love in these Psalms?

_____
_____
_____

Defining love

Love is pervasive in our time, not just in our music. Now let's look at how people think about love in our contemporary world. Think about the ways the word is used in every day language.

Check all the phrases below that are associated with love in our society:

Love is ...

- ◯ being physically attracted
- ◯ showing respect
- ◯ having empathy
- ◯ making someone happy
- ◯ receiving gifts from someone special
- ◯ receiving affection
- ◯ enjoying someone or something
- ◯ having an overwhelming obsession
- ◯ sexual activity

List any other phrases or concepts of love you have observed in society:

_____
_____
_____

Don't you love it! Love can refer to just about any kind of positive feeling or experience. Some of the phrases listed above refer to how people think about giving love as well as receiving love. It is sometimes conceived as a state of mind or emotion while at other times as active. Let's compare these many ways of conceiving of love in society with God's love.

In the video Chip provided this definition of the love of God:

> *God's love is His holy disposition toward all that He has created that compels Him to express unconditional affection and selective correction to provide the highest and best quality of existence both now and forever for the objects of His love.*

Describe some differences between the idea of love in society and the definition of God's love given by Chip:

_____

_____

_____

To be fair, love is a complex concept. Love is taking pleasure in another person such that it motivates actions that pursue the highest good of that person. That's what love is. But scriptures also provide us with descriptions of what love should look like in practice. Perhaps no Biblical portrayal of love is referenced more than Paul's description of love in 1 Corinthians 13. This passage paints a picture of what it looks like when someone pursues the good of another person rather than their own self-interest.

> *Love is patient, love is kind. It does not envy, it does not boast, it is not proud. It is not rude, it is not self-seeking, it is not easily angered, it keeps no record of wrongs. Love does not delight in evil but rejoices with the truth. It always protects, always trusts, always hopes, always perseveres. Love never fails.*
> **- 1 Corinthians 13:4-8**

This is real love. It's love that takes its pattern after God's love. Take a moment to consider how God relates to you in this way.

How have you experienced God treating you like the description in 1 Corinthians 13?

_____

_____

_____

In contrast, imagine having a relationship with someone who is:

- Impatient
- Mean-spirited
- Boastful
- Proud
- Rude
- Self-seeking
- Angry
- Holding a grudge
- Delighting in evil
- Unreliable

Imagine how different it is relating to someone who exhibits the qualities of 1 Corinthians 13 rather than the opposite qualities. It doesn't take much to realize that when a person exhibits 1 Corinthian 13 qualities, it changes everything. Consider how different the world would be if people did this more often.

What if people began to love each other just 50% more than they do now?

Which of the following do you think could be significantly impacted in our society by people being more loving to each other? *(Mark all that apply.)*

○ Depression

○ Loneliness

○ Addiction

○ Domestic abuse

○ Poverty

○ Homelessness

How would people being more loving have a positive impact on these issues?

Acts of Love

While 1 Corinthians 13 gives us a rich picture of godly love, you might be wanting to see something even more concrete as an example of God's love. Remember what Jesus told His disciples when Philip asked Him to show them the Father:

> *Philip said, "Lord, show us the Father and that will be enough for us." Jesus answered: "Don't you know me, Philip, even after I have been among you such a long time? Anyone who has seen me has seen the Father. How can you say, 'Show us the Father'? Don't you believe that I am in the Father, and that the Father is in me? The words I say to you are not just my own. Rather, it is the Father, living in me, who is doing his work. Believe me when I say that I am in the Father and the Father is in me."*
> **- John 14:8-11**

So, in order to see God's love at work let's take a look at two concrete acts of love from the life of Christ.

In John's gospel, a transition occurs at the beginning of chapter 13. The chapter begins with the statement:

> *It was just before the Passover Festival. Jesus knew that the hour had come for him to leave this world and go to the Father. Having loved his own who were in the world, he loved them to the end*
> **- John 13:1**

Washing Feet

What follows is a description of Jesus loving His own "to the end." John is describing the last moments that Jesus will spend with His disciples before He goes to His death on the cross. The first scene in this final movement of Christ's life begins by Jesus rising from the dinner table.

> *He got up from the meal, took off his outer clothing, and wrapped a towel around his waist. After that, he poured water into a basin and began to wash his disciples' feet, drying them with the towel that was wrapped around him.*
> **- John 13:4-5**

Why did Jesus do this?

He told them why.

> *Now that I, your Lord and Teacher, have washed your feet, you also should wash one another's feet. I have set you an example that you should do as I have done for you.*
> **- John 13:14-15**

Shortly afterwards, Jesus tells them:

> *Love one another. As I have loved you, so you must love one another*
> **- John 13:34**

How is Jesus' example of washing feet showing the disciples how to love?

_____

_____

_____

Before concluding the time with His disciples in the upper room and proceeding to His greatest act of love, John records Jesus' closing prayer to His Father:

> *I have made you known to them, and will continue to make you known in order that the love you have for me may be in them and that I myself may be in them.*
> **- John 17:26**

At this critical time, love remains at the forefront of Christ's mind.

Washing Away Sin

As Jesus leaves the upper room, He plunges into a long night that will lead to death by crucifixion the next day. He made reference to what He was about to do back in the upper room:

> *My command is this: Love each other as I have loved you. Greater love has no one than this: to lay down one's life for one's friends.*
> **- John 15:12-13**

Christ's work at the cross, then, is the greatest act of love the world will ever know.

These two acts—the washing of the feet and washing away the sins of the world with His blood—are the bookends of John's account of Jesus loving the disciples to the end. God's humble and sacrificial love gives itself for the good of the beloved.

Tough Love

We have seen how God's love has no bounds. He gave even the life of His Son. What cost Him more than we can imagine, He gave us freely. Now on the other side of salvation, what does God's love look like?

As we discussed in the chapter on the holiness of God, His vision for our lives is to make us holy. This is consistent with His love, since growing in holiness leads to the very best quality of life for us. It leads to intimacy with God. It leads to godly character. It leads to abundant life. But as we discussed in the chapter on the justice of God, our lives are far from being holy.

Therefore, like a parent who trains up a child in love, so God parents us in love:

> *My son, do not despise the LORD's discipline and do not resent his rebuke, because the LORD disciplines those he loves, as a father the son he delights in.*
> **- Proverbs 3:11-12**

List a few of the ways that God has shown his love to you in the past in the form of discipline? Looking back, can you also describe why it was for your good?

_____

_____

_____

His love will also allow other kinds of difficulty. But difficulty is something He uses to help us grow into maturity. This includes the trials and suffering that He allows:

> *Consider it pure joy, my brothers, whenever you face trials of many kinds, because you know that the testing of your faith develops perseverance. Perseverance must finish its work so that you may be mature and complete, not lacking anything.*
> **- James 1:2-4**

List a few of the ways that God has shown his love to you in the past by allowing you to face trials or suffering? Looking back, can you also describe how God worked good in your life through the experience? *(If God has still not revealed to you how He used it for your good, don't be concerned. Sometimes that understanding takes time or perhaps will not be known clearly until after life on earth.)*

_____

_____

_____

Thus, the love of God may not always feel like love. However, just like a parent who disciplines or who allows the child to face challenges, God pursues the good of those He loves through it all.

The Uniqueness of the Love of God

In this study we have been looking at attributes of God. We have said that God has the attributes of: goodness, sovereignty, holiness, wisdom, and justice. Those are all characteristics of God. We can trust that God will always exhibit those qualities. In this chapter we have been exploring the relationship between God and love. While we can also trust that God will always be loving, there is something unique about the love of God.

Our first clue to this is the observation that the Bible never states, "God is wisdom." Nor does it tell us, "God is holiness." Love is unique among the attributes in that scriptures tell us, "God is love." John, among all the disciples, saw first hand history's greatest act of love when Jesus gave up His life on the cross. Later in life and inspired by the Holy Spirit, here is what he said about the love of God:

> *Dear friends, let us love one another, for love comes from God. Everyone who loves has been born of God and knows God. Whoever does not love does not know God, because God is love. This is how God showed his love among us: He sent his one and only Son into the world that we might live through him. This is love: not that we loved God, but that he loved us and sent his Son as an atoning sacrifice for our sins.*
> *Dear friends, since God so loved us, we also ought to love one another. No one has ever seen God; but if we love one another, God lives in us and his love is made complete in us.*
>
> *This is how we know that we live in him and he in us: He has given us of his Spirit. And we have seen and testify that the Father has sent his Son to be the Savior of the world. If anyone acknowledges that Jesus is the Son of God, God lives in them and they in God. And so we know and rely on the love God has for us.*
>
> *God is love. Whoever lives in love lives in God, and God in them. This is how love is made complete among us so that we will have confidence on the day of judgment: In this world we are like Jesus. There is no fear in love. But perfect love drives out fear.*
> **- 1 John 4:7-18**

Below describe three things you observe about the love of God from these verses in 1 John 4:

1. _____
2. _____
3. _____

God's Love in Your Life

In the book of Revelation, Jesus writes letters to seven churches. In the letter to the church in Ephesus, He urges them to remember their first love (Revelation 2:4). Our love for Him is not the same as His love for us because our love for God can grow cold. Sometimes we don't experience God's love like we did before.

What is one thing you will do this week to open yourself to experience God's love afresh?

_____
_____
_____

The love we experience in relationship with God, both receiving His love and loving Him in return is central to the Christian life. The greatest of all commands states our obligation to love plainly:

> *"Teacher, which is the greatest commandment in the Law?"*
> *Jesus replied: "'Love the Lord your God with all your heart and with all your soul and with all your mind.' This is the first and greatest commandment. And the second is like it: 'Love your neighbor as yourself.'"*
> **- Matthew 22:36-39**

As Jesus makes clear, love for God and love for others are bound up together. The apostle John is blunt about the matter:

> *If anyone says, "I love God," yet hates his brother, he is a liar. For anyone who does not love his brother, whom he has seen, cannot love God, whom he has not seen. And he has given us this command: Whoever loves God must also love his brother.*
> **- 1 John 4:20-21**

What can we do to follow the pattern of loving others as Christ loved us? The opportunity to die for the good of another person is not so common. However, his example of humble service through washing the disciples' feet is much more relevant for every day life. And so is the picture we saw in 1 Corinthians 13.

Is there someone you have been neglecting that you believe God wants to love through you? What is one thing you can do this week to serve and care for that person?

_____

_____

_____

Is there a relationship in your life that has become so routine so that your relationship is merely going through the motions? What can you do this week to more actively, and in new ways, demonstrate love to that person?

_____

_____

_____

In conclusion, the love of God is an aspect of who He is that can never be exhausted. It is an exploration that brings great joy and depth to our relationship with Him. Let's finish with the apostle Paul's encouragement and His prayer both for the believers in Ephesus, but also for us:

> *And I pray that you, being rooted and established in love, may have power, together with all the saints, to grasp how wide and long and high and deep is the love of Christ, and to know this love that surpasses knowledge--that you may be filled to the measure of all the fullness of God.*
> **- Ephesians 3: 17-19**

CHAPTER **EIGHT**
Faithfulness of God

Your word, Lord, is eternal; it stands firm in the heavens.
Your faithfulness continues through all generations;
you established the earth, and it endures.

Psalm 119:89-90

A Friend Who Will be There for You

A friend is someone who is there when you are in greatest need. The best friends are also the people with whom we want to share life's special moments. Friendship is one of the most meaningful and fulfilling things we can experience.

The primacy of friendship in human experience has been widely recognized. Friendship has been the topic of some of the best literature, theatre, poetry, music, and films. The list is virtually limitless. Here are just a few famous examples from literature:
- Achilles and Patroclus in Homer's Iliad
- Tom Sawyer and Huck Finn in Mark Twain's *The Adventures of Tom Sawyer*
- Anne Shirley and Diana Barry in L. M. Montgomery's *Anne of Green Gables*
- Sherlock Holmes and John Watson in Sir Arthur Conan Doyle's *Sherlock Holmes* series
- Aibileen and Minny in Kathryn Stockett's *The Help*

We all have had moments in life when we need someone to come through for us. Think about various kinds of life circumstances when you would most want a friend to "be there" for you and with you.

Rank these circumstances in order of the ones you would most want a friend to support you or experience with you: *(Rank 1-5 with 1 being the circumstance you most would want a friend.)*

_____ Your wedding

_____ Loss of a loved one

_____ Birth of a child

_____ Loss of your job

_____ Road trip or vacation

_____ Hospitalization

_____ Other: _____

_____ Other: _____

What you have undoubtedly found is that no matter how faithful, no friend is able to be there for you 100% of the time in the way you need a friend. Nor will you be able to be a friend to others 100% of the time. Yet, as Chip will discuss, we desperately need someone or something to come through for us at all times and places or else we face great insecurity and anxiety in life. Let's see how God is ready and willing to be more faithful than the best of friends at all times.

CHAPTER EIGHT

> **VIDEO** — Watch Chip Ingram's Teaching and fill in the notes below.
>
> ### ▶ The Faithfulness of God

1. We all depend on something or someone to "hold us up" inside.

2. When that something or someone is "coming through for us," we experience a sense of peace, satisfaction, and optimism about the future.

3. When that something or someone "fails to come through for us," we experience a sense of anxiety, dissatisfaction, and ultimately despair.

Conclusion: It seems that the secret to life is to find something or someone who will "come through for you" 100% of the time in any and every situation forever.

The Solution = Lamentations 3:21-23

Defining the Faithfulness of God

Definition: Steadfast in affection or allegiance (loyal).
Synonyms: Dependable, trustworthy, loyal, staunch, resolute, constant, reliable, true to one's word, keeps one's promises, someone "who comes through for you."

Why is God Able to be Faithful 100% of the Time?

1. He is **all-knowing** – He is never caught off guard. *Romans 11:33-36*

2. He is **all-powerful** – He never encounters anything or anyone who can thwart His plans or purposes.

3. He is **holy** – He is pure, honest, full of integrity, unable to lie, and there, is always consistent with His character and His Word. *Isaiah 6:1-6*

4. He is **eternal** – He is not affected by space or time; He knows the end from the beginning. *Psalm 90:2*

5. He is **omnipresent** – Nothing can happen outside the sphere of His influence.
   – *Psalm 139:7-11*

6. He is **immutable** – He never changes, is never different than He is now, is never in a bad mood, and never has a bad day. – *Malachi 3:6; Hebrews 13:8*

> *All of God's acts are consistent with all of His attributes. No attribute contradicts any other, but all harmonize and blend into each other in the infinite abyss of the Godhead...He is at once faithful and immutable, so all His words and acts must be and must remain faithful.*
> **- A.W. Tozer**

Summary: God is 100% faithful to His Word, His promises, His people, and His character because He cannot be otherwise. He will never let you down!

God Reveals His Faithfulness to Us Through…

- His _____ *Psalm 119:89-90; 145:13-16*

- His _____
  - The Patriarchs *Genesis 12:1-3*
  - David *Psalm 132:11*
  - The Church *Matthew 16:18*

- His _____
  - The Father *Numbers 23:19*
  - The Spirit *Galatians 5:23*
  - The Son *Revelation 19:11 - 16*

- His _____ *Isaiah 55:10 - 11*
  - His Word is true *John 17:17*
  - He keeps His covenants *Deuteronomy 7:9*
  - He keeps His promises *Hebrews 10:23*
  - He fulfills His predictions *Isaiah 42:8-10*

- His _____ of our lives when…
  - We are weak *2 Corinthians 12:9-10*
  - We are tempted *1 Corinthians 10:13*
  - We sin *1 John 1:9*
  - We utterly fail *2 Timothy 2:11-13*

How Can We Respond to God's Faithfulness?

7. Put your _____ behind you today!

   If we confess our sins, He is faithful and just and will forgive us our sins and purify us from all unrighteousness.
   1 John 1:9

8. Bring your _____ problems, pains, and failures to Jesus today!

   Come to me, all you who are weary and burdened, and I will give you rest. Take my yoke upon you and learn from me, for I am gentle and humble in heart, and you will find rest for your souls. For my yoke is easy and my burden is light.
   Matthew 11:28-30

9. Place your _____ for the future in the One who will never let you down!

   This is what the Lord says:

   "Cursed is the one who trusts in man, who draws strength from mere flesh and whose heart turns away from the Lord. That person will be like a bush in the wastelands; they will not see prosperity when it comes. They will dwell in the parched places of the desert, in a salt land where no one lives. "But blessed is the one who trusts in the Lord, whose confidence is in him. They will be like a tree planted by the water that sends out its roots by the stream. It does not fear when heat comes; its leaves are always green. It has no worries in a year of drought and never fails to bear fruit." Jeremiah 17:5-8

The Faithfulness of God

The following questions will help you reflect on what you watched on the video. If you are in a group spend some time sharing with others.

1. What are some examples in the Bible where God showed His faithfulness to someone? God was faithful to them, share where you have failed and God was faithful to you.

2. In what ways do we see the attribute of faithfulness manifested in the life of Jesus? List specific instances and the words of Jesus to support your observations.

3. 1 Corinthians 10:13 (NIV) says, *"No temptation has overtaken you except what is common to mankind. And God is faithful; he will not let you be tempted beyond what you can bear. But when you are tempted, he will also provide a way out so that you can endure it."*

   - How is God faithful when we find ourselves being tempted?

4. In 2 Corinthians 12:9-10 (NIV) Paul says But he said to me, "My grace is sufficient for you, for my power is made perfect in weakness." Therefore I will boast all the more gladly about my weaknesses, so that Christ's power may rest on me. 10 That is why, for Christ's sake, I delight in weaknesses, in insults, in hardships, in persecutions, in difficulties. For when I am weak, then I am strong.

   - In the past, how have you seen God be faithful in a time of weakness?

5. Read Lamentations 3:21-24. What word or phrase most stands out to you? Why?

6. What circumstances are you going through that you need to trust in the faithfulness of God to? What does that look like practically? Be specific.

As you close this session, pray for one another to trust the faithfulness of God. As you intercede for your friends, pray the promises of God over each other.

NEXT STEPS

A Place to Remember God's Faithfulness

> *For the word of the LORD is right and true; he is faithful in all he does.*
> **- Psalm 33:4**

It was a day to remember. Some must have wondered if it ever would come to pass. They had heard stories from their parents about the wondrous miracles of God. The crossing of the Red Sea. The defeat of their Egyptian masters. The desert manna. Water gushing forth from a rock in a dry and parched land.

This day, the children of Israel would experience something that had been foretold and promised so many generations earlier. Their far distant ancestor Abraham had received the promise from God:

> *The LORD said to Abram after Lot had parted from him, "Lift up your eyes from where you are and look north and south, east and west. All the land that you see I will give to you and your offspring forever. I will make your offspring like the dust of the earth, so that if anyone could count the dust, then your offspring could be counted. Go, walk through the length and breadth of the land, for I am giving it to you."*
> **- Genesis 13:14-17**

Abraham would walk and see the land but would not possess it. He was merely a father with a large household. But the promise would be repeated to him (Genesis 15:7, 17:4-8). It was as if the title to the land had been given to him by God, but full possession would have to wait until later.

The promise was repeated and remembered. God reassured Isaac:

> *I will make your descendants as numerous as the stars in the sky and will give them all these lands, and through your offspring all nations on earth will be blessed.*
> **- Genesis 26:4**

Joseph, two generations later, reminded the children of Abraham on his deathbed that God would be true to His Word:

> *Then Joseph said to his brothers, "I am about to die. But God will surely come to your aid and take you up out of this land to the land he promised on oath to Abraham, Isaac and Jacob."*
> **- Genesis 50:24**

God does not forget his promises. Some three hundred years after Joseph, the children of Abraham then living as slaves in Egypt surely must have doubted the old "stories" about being given the land of the Canaanites. But God spoke again, this time to Moses:

> *"Go, assemble the elders of Israel and say to them, 'The LORD, the God of your fathers—the God of Abraham, Isaac and Jacob—appeared to me and said: I have watched over you and have seen what has been done to you in Egypt. And I have promised to bring you up out of your misery in Egypt into the land of the Canaanites, Hittites, Amorites, Perizzites, Hivites and Jebusites—a land flowing with milk and honey.'"*
> **- Exodus 3:16-17**

After a roller coaster ride in the desert between Egypt and Canaan, God faithfully brought forth a nation prepared to possess the land. He had been faithful to provide for their needs, to give them instructions for their good, and to be present with them in a pillar of cloud by day and of fire by night. Those offspring of Abraham, now a great multitude of descendants, stood at the shore of the Jordan. God was about to fulfill His promise.

It's hard to imagine how meaningful and humbling it must have been to experience that long awaited moment of entering in—as a nation ready to possess their promised land.

God did not want this moment to be soon forgotten. He instructed Joshua to pick one man from each tribe:

> *"Choose twelve men from among the people, one from each tribe, and tell them to take up twelve stones from the middle of the Jordan from right where the priests stood and to carry them over with you and put them down at the place where you stay tonight."*
> **- Joshua 4:2-3**

Then God made the purpose of this exercise clear to them:

> *He said to the Israelites, "In the future when your descendants ask their fathers, 'What do these stones mean?' tell them, 'Israel crossed the Jordan on dry ground.' For the LORD your God dried up the Jordan before you until you had crossed over. The LORD your God did to the Jordan just what he had done to the Red Sea when he dried it up before us until we had crossed over. He did this so that all the peoples of the earth might know that the hand of the LORD is powerful and so that you might always fear the LORD your God."*
> - **Joshua 4:21-24**

These stones were meant to be "a memorial forever" to the people of Israel (Joshua 4:7). They would forever remind the Israelites that God was willing, able, and faithful to fulfill His promise, even if it seemed to take a long time in the perspective of human beings.

What special place(s) is a reminder of God's faithfulness to you?

_____

_____

Why is this a place of remembrance of God's faithfulness for you?

_____

_____

An Old Testament Pairing: God's Faithfulness and Love

It's not surprising that the later generations of Israelites would sing of God's faithfulness. What is interesting is how often the divinely inspired songs of the Israelites captured in the book of Psalms pair God's faithfulness with His love. Here are just a few examples:

> *Your love, O LORD, reaches to the heavens, your faithfulness to the skies.*
> - **Psalm 36:5**

> *For great is your love, reaching to the heavens; your faithfulness reaches to the skies.*
> **- Psalm 57:10**

> *But you, O Lord, are a compassionate and gracious God, slow to anger, abounding in love and faithfulness.*
> **- Psalm 86:15**

> *I will sing of the LORD's great love forever; with my mouth I will make your faithfulness known through all generations.*
>
> *I will declare that your love stands firm forever, that you established your faithfulness in heaven itself.*
> **- Psalm 89:1-2**

Why do you think that the psalmist so often link faithfulness and love?

_____

_____

_____

In the story of Abraham and his descendants it's clear that God was 100% faithful. He showed himself not only willing but also able to be faithful. In the video Chip discussed some of the reasons why God is faithful 100% of the time for each and every one of us. We're going to explore in more detail how it is that God is able to be absolutely faithful and how that impacts our lives.

The Faithfulness of God in Difficult Life Circumstances

Take some time now to consider God's ability to be faithful in the light of various personal life circumstances you face. We know that God is completely reliable because He is...

All-knowing (Romans 11:33-36)

- God knows all things.

  What might God know about you or your current circumstances that assures you that He is able to come through for you?

  Confusing or difficult life situations: _____

All-powerful (Hebrews 1:3)

- God has power over all things.

  What kinds of opposition or obstacles do you face right now in which you are comforted by knowing that they are not beyond the control of God?

  Opposition or obstacles in your life:: _____

Morally perfect (Isaiah 6:1-6)

- God is good, not deceiving or malevolent. There is no darkness or evil in God at all.

  What injustices in our world might make you feel vulnerable, insecure, or despairing if you knew that God was not holy and morally perfect?

  Injustices: _____

Eternal (Psalm 90:2)

- No future events are unknown or uncertain to God.

  What kinds of deadlines or upcoming events are approaching that might make you anxious, except for the calming effect of trusting in a God for whom the future is not unknown or uncertain?

  Future uncertainties: _____

Everywhere present (Psalm 139:7-11)

- God is not limited by place or space. No place is outside His sovereignty.

  What places are most troubling to you, except when you remember and trust that God is there with you?

  Troubling places: _____

Unchanging (Malachi 3:6; Hebrews 13:8)

- God is not fickle or undecided. He does not change His mind or His character.

    What are some of the things in your life that are constantly changing and uncertain in the midst of which God's unchanging character provides you with stability and security?

    Constantly changing life dynamics: _____

As you look back over your answers to the series of questions on the previous pages describe the difference it can make when you face your life circumstances knowing that God is completely reliable in His unshakeable faithfulness to you:

_____

_____

The Faithfulness of God in Personal Relationship

The previous section directed us to take comfort in God's faithfulness in light of all the difficulties we might face living in a broken and uncertain world. He is faithful to protect us and provide us with the security we so desperately need.

However, God's faithfulness not only shields from the uncertainties and evil around us. His faithfulness is demonstrated in the very personal way that He engages with us in relationship:

- He **strengthens** His people.

> *But the Lord is faithful, and he will strengthen and protect you from the evil one.*
> **- 2 Thessalonians 3:3**

- He is **present** with His people.

> *And I will ask the Father, and he will give you another Counselor to be with you forever—the Spirit of truth. The world cannot accept him, because it neither sees him nor knows him. But you know him, for he lives with you and will be in you.*
> **- John 14:16-17**

> *Keep your lives free from the love of money and be content with what you have, because God has said, "Never will I leave you; never will I forsake you."*
> **- Hebrews 13:5**

- He **matures** His people and makes them holy.

> *May God himself, the God of peace, sanctify you through and through. May your whole spirit, soul and body be kept blameless at the coming of our Lord Jesus Christ. The one who calls you is faithful and he will do it.*
> **- 1 Thessalonians 5:23-24**

To what degree are you currently experiencing God's faithfulness in each of these three categories: *(Rating is 5 for the most prevalent and 1 for the least. NOTE: God is faithful in all these categories at all times. However, at different times we have a greater awareness of His faithful work in these ways.)*

Strengthening you

1 ──── 2 ──── 3 ──── 4 ──── 5
○   ○   ○   ○   ○

Being present with you

1 ──── 2 ──── 3 ──── 4 ──── 5
○   ○   ○   ○   ○

Maturing you

1 ──── 2 ──── 3 ──── 4 ──── 5
○   ○   ○   ○   ○

Why do you think you are experiencing His faithfulness more in some ways now than in other ways?

_____

_____

_____

A Communion to Remember God's Faithfulness

Many generations after the Israelites entered into the Promised Land through the Jordan River, a group of frightened and uncertain young men sat in an upper room in Jerusalem. They were celebrating God's faithfulness to their ancestors who God brought out of Egyptian slavery. They were observing the Passover. And they were wondering what would become of all the heightened tension building around their beloved Jesus. What they didn't realize is that He was about to deliver on another age-old promise of God. It was an even more significant promise—the promise to bless all people.

This Jesus, who they had given up everything to follow, broke bread and took a cup of wine. As He shared these with His disciples, He stated His intentions:

> *And he took bread, gave thanks and broke it, and gave it to them, saying, "This is my body given for you; do this in remembrance of me." In the same way, after the supper he took the cup, saying, "This cup is the new covenant in my blood, which is poured out for you."*
> - Luke 22:19-20

When we share the bread and the cup some two thousand years later, we remember the faithfulness of God. His faithfulness to redeem us through His Son. His faithfulness to provide a sacrifice that forever wipes away our sins. His faithfulness to clothe us in the righteousness of His Son.

Describe how your participation in communion has been a reminder of God's faithfulness to you:

_____

_____

_____

Jesus was faithful to go to the cross for our salvation. He left this world, but left us with the Holy Spirit. The Spirit's life in us is a guarantee of God's ownership of us and a coming time of complete renewal:

> *For while we are in this tent, we groan and are burdened, because we do not wish to be unclothed but to be clothed with our heavenly dwelling, so that what is mortal may be swallowed up by life. Now it is God who has made us for this very purpose and has given us the Spirit as a deposit, guaranteeing what is to come.*
> **- 2 Corinthians 5:4-5**

We can trust that He will be faithful to bring this to pass, just as He was faithful to bring the Israelites into their promised land. Just as the Son was faithful to the will of the Father—"who for the joy set before him endured the cross, scorning its shame" (Hebrews 12:2)—we know our salvation is assured. We are encouraged by the apostle John who shared a vision that God gave him at the end of his long life—Jesus will indeed prove Himself faithful. John saw a vision of the promised return of his friend, his Savior and his God. The Lord Jesus Christ will indeed judge the world and usher in a new era of righteousness and justice:

> *I saw heaven standing open and there before me was a white horse, whose rider is called Faithful and True.*
> **- Revelation 19:11**

God's Faithfulness In Your Life

For the Israelites who passed through the Jordan, that pile of stones taken from the bottom of the Jordan was a symbol of remembrance. What they remembered was the faithfulness of God to fulfill His promises. It reminded them of His power and will to come through for His people.

One of the greatest ways that our faith grows and is strengthened is through remembrance of God's past work in our lives. Recalling those moments in life when you knew with certainty that God was coming through for you, helps your faith to be strengthened in the present.

In the chart on the next page, describe five past events or periods of time in your life that God came through for you in a dramatic or important way.

Then, answer how do these remembrances strengthen your confidence in God's faithfulness with a difficult situation you are facing in life right now?

Five past events from your life	How God's faithfulness strengthens your confidence

CONCLUSION

*I will sing of your love and justice;
to you, O LORD, I will sing praise..*

Psalm 101:1

Reviewing Your Study of the Real God

In this study you have faced the challenge of getting to know the God and Creator of the universe. He is altogether different from us and beyond our full comprehension. And yet He desires for us to know about Him to the degree that we can. Additionally, He wants us to know Him personally. He proactively initiates relationship with us.

We have attempted to get to know Him as much as we can given our limitations. In order to help ourselves in this quest, we have discussed several of His qualities: goodness, sovereignty, holiness, wisdom, justice, love, and faithfulness. This is fine as far as it goes. However, it is critical that we realize that this approach is also limited. We must not conclude that God is the sum of those parts or attributes. In this study we have merely approached God and begun to see Him with a bit more focused clarity. We have not gotten to know God in His entirety. Not by a long shot.

Another limitation to our study is that we have not explored in much depth the relationships between these seven attributes. On several occasions relationships between them have come up, but that is just the tip of the iceberg. These attributes of God are intricately intertwined. A short selection of verses reveal just how intertwined they are:

> *Righteousness and justice are the foundation of your throne; love and faithfulness go before you.*
> **- Psalm 89:14**

> *For the LORD is good and his love endures forever; his faithfulness continues through all generations.*
> **- Psalm 100:5**

> *I will sing of your love and justice; to you, O LORD, I will sing praise.*
> **- Psalm 101:1**

This is a crucial point. The attributes of God are always in harmony and never at odds. Sometimes understanding the harmony between them is challenging, and yet necessary to have a clear picture of who God is. Imagine, for example, if God somehow took off His justice when He was being loving. What would it look like if God could be loving but not just? What would it look like if God could be just but not loving?

CHAPTER CONCLUSION

Thankfully, God is both just and loving. Unfortunately we don't have time to go into exploring the insights we could gain from exploring the many relationships between His attributes. But that gives you an opportunity to engage in many studies on your own!

This highlights an important takeaway point of this study that we hope you have noticed. There is no limit getting to know God better. We saw that with His love, but it's true of all His attributes. We can explore the depths and heights of His love and never reach a top or a bottom. You can forever be more and more filled with the fullness of God as you get to know Him more and more.

Capturing Your Learning

Before concluding this study, we owe it to ourselves to assess our learning and identify some key points and action steps to take with us.

The Four Evidences of Knowing God

To evaluate your learning in this study, we're returning to J.I. Packer's four evidences of knowing God from Chapter 1. Use the chart below to rate yourself in the four evidences (10 being highest, 1 being lowest).

	Rating (1-10)
Amount of energy for God *Those who really know God take action and demonstrate initiative both in public and private as a result of knowing Him.*	
Greatness of thoughts about God *Those who really know God fill their minds often with awe-inspiring reminders of God's greatness.*	
Degree of boldness for God *Those who really know God don't hesitate to obey by faith even when it might cost them.*	
Level of contentment in God *Those who really know God experience peace even in the midst of trying circumstances.*	

How did the some of the things you learned about God impact your ratings above?

_____

_____

Five Principles and Three Action Steps

This final exercise will have you looking back through your workbook. Go back through the workbook and identify five principles and three action steps that you want to emphasize in your thinking and in your behavior as you leave this study behind.

Each of the five principles should be a single statement. One might be as simple as copying a verse that God has continued to bring to your mind of one or more of His attributes. It could be a quotation from a workbook chapter, from Chip, or from another author. Or it could be something you observed or wrote down in your notes. The statement you write should be a strong reminder to you of who God is.

Five Principles

1. _____

2. _____

3. _____

4. _____

5. _____

CHAPTER CONCLUSION

As for the three action steps, go back through the chapters and choose three that you want to incorporate into your life on a consistent basis. Perhaps you want to modify how you apply the steps to your life, but make it a point to build these into your daily habits.

Three Action Steps

1. _____

2. _____

3. _____

Incorporate the lessons you have learned about God into your life every day. Think about Him when you rise up in the morning and when you lay down to sleep at night—and at every moment in between. There is no better object of our attention and study than God Himself. May He richly bless you as you get to know Him more and more for who He really is!

Notes

Notes

Notes

Notes